Who is Barry Goldwater? What is his personal and political background? What does he stand for? How did he win the Republican Presidential nomination? Most important, is he a "prisoner" of the Radical Right, or a willing collaborator in its drive for power?

The answers to these and other questions about Goldwater—the man, the myth, the menace—are in this informative, detailed, and up-to-the-minute analysis.

THE AUTHOR

Three-time winner of the New York Newspaper Guild's Page One Award, Fred J. Cook is the author of fifteen books and many hundreds of articles on a wide range of social and political topics. In 1960, he co-authored the widely hailed special issue of *The Nation*, "The Shame of New York." He won the 1961 Sidney Hillman Award with *The Warfare State*, a Book Find Club selection that attracted world-wide attention. His most recent book is *The FBI Nobody Knows* (Macmillan).

BARRY GOLDWATER

Extremist of the Right

Fred J. Cook

An Evergreen Black Cat *Book*

Grove Press, Inc.   New York

Contents

CHAPTER I

The Takeover

The enormous Cow Palace in San Francisco vibrated with sound, quivered with passion. Streamers waved, placards did a crazy dance, drums thundered as for tribal war, and balloons released in a triumphant barrage drifted down like giant snowflakes in a blizzard. Dominating all, the center of the cyclone of noise and confusion and emotion, stood a tall, handsome, gray-haired man with an eagle profile, strong nose, iron jaw and wide, firm, mobile lips.

Barry Morris Goldwater, at 55, had been nominated for the Presidency of the United States at the Republican National Convention, and he was now on this evening of July 16, 1964 about to deliver his acceptance speech — a speech that would be long remembered for the heavily underscored lines: "Extremism in defense of liberty is no vice; moderation in the pursuit of justice is no virtue."

Those words — words that would cause his audience to erupt in a shout of approbation — had not been spoken yet. For the moment, in the din, it was impossible to speak. Former Vice President Richard M. Nixon, who had introduced the nominee, grabbed Goldwater's wrist, and together they stood, arms extended and uplifted in the traditional gesture of the victor. Goldwater's wide lips split in a grin of triumph that sent his right-wing followers into a fresh burst of frenzy, triggering emotion much as the famous battle grin of Franklin Roosevelt once had fired the liberal legions.

Across the nation millions sat with eyes riveted to their television screens, watching the pandemonium, feeling the fervor and passion quiver along their nerve ends, absorbed in the man whose figure at the moment cast its shadow over America.

Those with memories could recall another and almost identical scene, just four years previously at the Republican convention in Chicago. Then, too, for one lonely moment, Goldwater had stood in the spotlight, the cynosure of all eyes, the man in the eye of a storm of emotion.

But, between the two scenes, what a difference!

The Republican delegates had gone to Chicago in 1960 with their party's Presidential nomination predetermined. Richard M. Nixon had the votes, and any challenge to his candidacy had been doomed to failure. Still, for one brief and electric moment, the challenge had been mounted.

Arizona had advanced the name of Barry Goldwater. South Carolina, too, was in his camp. In other delegations there was a spattering of strength, and just prior to the convention, a group of far-out rightists had met in Chicago and had formed an organization known as Americans for Goldwater. Into Chicago had poured a following of young conservative zealots from across the nation, ready to shout and cheer and demonstrate for their hero.

But Barry Goldwater had recognized the futility of heading a forlorn charge up heights so securely held by the opposition. And so on July 27, 1960 he had made his way to the rostrum to withdraw his name from nomination. His appearance, his announced intention had touched off a wave of emotion and of protest foreshadowing events to come. As he began to speak, there welled up from the convention floor and cascaded down from the galleries a deep, hoarse roar of protest — "No!" The cry was taken up and repeated, resounding through the hall in an anguished chorus of "No, no, no!"

Goldwater had held up his hand, had obtained quiet, had launched into a brief appeal for party unity.

"We are conservatives," he had reminded his followers.

"This great Republican Party is our historic house.

"This is our *home* . . .

"We must remember that Republicans have not been losing elections because of more Democrat voters. We have been losing elections because conservatives too often fail to vote.

"I am a conservative.

"I am going to devote all my time — from now until November — to electing Republicans — from the top of the ticket — to the bottom of the ticket.

"I call upon my fellow conservatives to do the same."

He had finished to a roar of applause. Then he had turned

and left the podium, had vanished from the spotlight. But he had left an indelible impression. Handsome, bronzed and fit, a jet pilot and looking it, he had cast himself in the role of the good loser, of a man who placed principle and party loyalty above personal ambition. Across the nation he had registered on the television screens of millions with an impact new and forceful and almost wholly favorable. Just as Jack Kennedy had emerged from the 1956 Vice Presidential photo finish with Estes Kefauver as the personality boy in his party's future, so Barry Goldwater had impinged for the first time upon the consciousness of a national audience as the rising star of dedicated, conservative Republicanism.

Now, four years later in San Francisco, Barry Goldwater occupied the spotlight, but this time he would not so quickly depart. Now he was his party's nominee for the Presidency. Now, bitter primary campaigns and recriminations behind him, he was prepared to mount an ultra-conservative challenge to the policies of President Lyndon B. Johnson in the fall election campaign.

To his followers, to the fanatics of the Radical Right, his nomination represented a heady, incredible triumph. For twenty-four years, with growing frenzy and frustration, they had inveighed against their party's dominance by the Eastern, moderately liberal and internationalist wing of Republicanism. They had clamored for an end to "me-tooism"; they had proclaimed, and they passionately believed, the thesis that millions of affronted conservatives had sat on their hands every four years because they hadn't been offered a choice — that only the selection of a "true conservative" could assuage these silent protestors and lure their votes into the ballot box. Now these diehards of ultra-conservatism had their wish. Now they had their chosen knight to lead them in the showdown against what they regarded as the "radical" forces of liberalism. Now the event that it had seemed could never happen had happened — and entirely new forces had assumed control and direction of the Republican Party.

It was an event of historic significance, an event without parallel in the recent political history of the nation. Americans usually shun extremism in any form; but now extremists, symbolized by the John Birch Society, had seized the reins of Republicanism and had nominated their chosen candidate. Because they had, the nomination of Barry Goldwater meant different things to different people.

Across the breadth of America on this night of decision in

mid-July, 1964, Barry Goldwater was a symbol and a rallying point for the frustrated, no matter what the source of their frustration. For those impatient with the seemingly endless tensions and demands of the Cold War, he offered the anodyne of super-patriotism in the stirring cry, "Why Not Victory?" For those rebelling against the so-called "give-away" of billions in the foreign aid program, he was the champion of champions — for he would end it. For those resenting Negro aggressiveness in the civil rights battle, he was the hero and the beneficiary of the white "backlash" — for he had voted against the civil rights bill. For the wealthy galled by high income taxes, he was the potential saviour — for he had vowed the death of the progressive income tax just as soon as feasible. For businessmen rebelling against government "interference" and haunted by the specter of government "competition," he was the Sir Galahad who would dispose of the Tennessee Valley Authority, if only for $1, and cut back government programs everywhere. For all such, Barry Goldwater coalesced deep-lying impulses of frustration and rebellion; he was their man, the chosen of their heart's desire, and he represented the long-awaited and long-denied opportunity to prove at the polls the right-ness of their passionately professed rightism.

Others, millions of others, viewed the proceedings in San Francisco with emotions that ranged from doubt and skepticism to outright alarm. In varying degrees, depending on personal reactions to a broad spectrum of national issues, they saw the outwardly handsome and engaging man who occupied the podium of the Cow Palace as an impetuous and simple-minded blunderer in the age of nuclear tensions and mass complexities. They saw him as a trigger-happy, fast-draw artist with an alarming tendency to shoot from the hip and ask questions afterward. Here was a man who had proposed to send the Marines into Cuba to turn on the water, and to use an atom bomb to "defoliate" Vietnam. Here was a man who had emphatically repudiated the entire fabric of American government in the twentieth century (President Eisenhower once remarked that Goldwater was more then ninety years behind the times in his concept of governmental functions and spending); a man who fought against a higher minimum wage law, opposed medicare, decried Social Security, battled federal aid to education, rejected the idea of a Department of Urban Affairs or area redevelopment or federal improvement projects in any shape or form (unless they were billion-dollar reclamation projects for his own state of Arizona).

To millions of American voters, these stands made the face they saw on their television screen, however attractive, the face of reaction — a reaction that, in some stunning and mysterious fashion, had wrested control of one of the great political parties from the moderates who had ruled it ever since the nomination of Wendell Willkie in 1940. What made this takeover, this turn-about, most surprising was the simple fact that there seemed to have been no overwhelmingly popular mandate for such a drastic change.

Barry Goldwater was clearly the standard bearer of a minority, even within his own party, and he had triumphed in the face of much concrete evidence that he was a predestined loser. In January and February, he had taken his case into one of the nation's most conservative states, rock-ribbed Republican New Hampshire, where all the preliminary polls showed him to be the darling of the electorate as well as the hero of virtually all the state's leading politicians. Beginning his campaign under such favorable auspices, Goldwater had stormed up and down the state, expounding his right-wing doctrine in speech after speech, firing from the hip in impromptu newspaper interviews — and the result had been a stunning vote of disenchantment, the emphatic decision of the conservative New Hampshire electorate that they would much prefer a candidate whom they hadn't even seen or heard, Henry Cabot Lodge.

In Oregon, where Lodge initially seemed to have great strength, Goldwater had fought a rear-guard skirmish against New York's Gov. Nelson A. Rockefeller. And Rockefeller had drawn a sharp issue — "mainstream" Republicanism on the one side; the Radical Right on the other. Though handicapped by the sensitive issue of his divorce and remarriage, Rockefeller had nevertheless scored an upset. He had won; Lodge had come in second; and Goldwater had trailed.

It was a victory for an underdog that had seemed to say the voters of the Pacific Northwest endorsed a moderate liberalism, vetoed any Radical Right extremism. But then had come California, the nation's most populous state and the primary that pitted Rockefeller and Goldwater, just the two of them, in head-on battle. The dedicated Radical Rightists in the Southern and most populous section of the state had gone all-out for their champion, and with their help Goldwater had defeated Rockefeller in the one test of strength that he simply had to win, capturing California's bloc of 86 convention votes — and, with them, a virtual stranglehold on the Republican nomination.

June had seen the entry into the race of Governor William W. Scranton, of Pennsylvania, in a desperate, eleventh-hour effort to halt the Goldwater bandwagon. Scranton's belated entry after months of fence-sitting had been inspired by two principal factors — Goldwater's vote against the civil rights bill, which in Scranton's view was an affront to the party of Lincoln, and a galloping case of the most abysmal blue funk that afflicted Scranton's friends and fellow Republican officeholders confronted with the imminent reality of seeking re-election under the aegis of Goldwater's Birch-like rightism. Throughout the populous industrial states of the East and Midwest, Republican candidates who had to face their electorates in November frankly confessed they feared unmitigated disaster.

Public opinion polls demonstrated that they had legitimate cause for concern. In late June, with the Republican convention less than three weeks away, polls limited to Republican voters only showed the depth of the popular distaste and distrust of Goldwater's extremist candidacy. In Ohio, heartland of Taft conservatism, one poll showed that no fewer than 64 percent of Republican voters planned to support President Johnson; only 17 percent declared for Goldwater — and 19 percent were undecided. In Iowa, where Republicanism flourishes like the tall corn, 50 percent of Republicans plumped for President Johnson, 36 percent for Goldwater — and 14 percent were undecided. Significantly, a full half of the Republicans who said they were going to vote for Johnson declared they were doing so simply because they couldn't vote for Goldwater and what he stood for.

These were trends that were repeated with unmistakable consistency in state after state throughout the nation. What they said was plain: Goldwater was clearly the choice of only a minority within his own party, and his party, except when led by war-hero Eisenhower, had been a minority party. And so on this night of choice, standing in the glare of lights on the Cow Palace podium, erect and handsome and personally appealing in the full view of television's seeing-eye, Barry Goldwater was a figure shrouded in doubt, in controversy, in the malaise of deep divisions within his own party about the meaning of the American way and the direction of the American dream.

Yet he was his party's candidate for the Presidency. The Birchites and their Radical Rightist brethren, who stood in the wings behind him, only half-concealed by the aura of his personal magnetism, had indeed achieved the seemingly impossible — they had turned back the clock, they had captured the party of Lincoln, they had dictated the choice of a Presidential candidate.

How had it happened? And what did it mean — for the present and for the future?

Those were the questions that millions of Americans throughout the land were asking themselves on this night of irrevocable decision. The answers were to be found in the life and career of Barry Goldwater — and in the record of the men and forces behind him.

CHAPTER II

The Kickoff

The way it started tells much about the man and his candidacy. In making his formal announcement on January 3, 1964, Barry Goldwater proclaimed he would give the voters "a choice, not an echo."

There had been little doubt since 1960 that the junior United States Senator from Arizona was in the race for the Republican Presidential nomination — and running hard. But Goldwater, ever the consummate politician, had played it coy. Ardent supporters were drumming up all this talk about his candidacy, he had said. It was a grass roots movement, and he couldn't stop it. He would just have to let it go and see how far it got. This disarming pose charmed many knowledgeable commentators into the belief that Goldwater really didn't want to run, but was being shoved along by an ultra-conservative wave too strong for him to resist. A long and consistent chain of events, beginning even before the 1960 defeat of Nixon, would seem to indicate that this was not so, that Goldwater was no reluctant dragon; and when the moment of truth finally arrived, it brought with it much intrinsic evidence that Barry Goldwater is a strong-willed and obdurate man who isn't going to be led or shoved any place he doesn't want to go.

The manner in which he elected to pitch his hat into the ring spoke volumes, for it involved a series of decisions in which he overruled the advice of his personal brain trust. Goldwater had just had an operation for the removal of a bone spur on one heel. His foot was in a cast. He had to hobble on crutches. Therefore, his aides advised that he wait a few days. What would a few days' delay matter? And why begin running for the Presidency on crutches? Goldwater heeded none of the arguments. He had decided on January 3, and January 3 it would be.

The date happened to fall on a Friday. Now, as every newsman knows, Saturday's papers are the week's worst read. Advisers pointed out to Goldwater that Theodore Roosevelt had feathered his publicity nest by timing his pronouncements on Sunday so that they could make the Monday morning papers. Monday papers, the astute Teddy had discovered, were always starving for news, and so any kind of worthwhile tid-bit could be almost guaranteed a place on the front pages. Goldwater listened, but was not dissuaded. Friday it would be.

The site of the momentous announcement caused another debate. Washington, with all its available communications facilities, seemed like the logical place, but Goldwater would have none of it. He was determined to make his declaration on his home turf. In Phoenix, then? His staff pointed out that a place like the Westward Ho in Phoenix could accommodate the reporters, the television crews, the vast publicity mob that would swarm to the occasion. No, said Goldwater, he would do the deed on his own patio.

The result was that newsmen and communications crews all trekked out to Paradise City, an expensive ranch-house suburb in the hills looking down on Phoenix. The village itself perches in scrub and desert country. A road climbs up from the desert, and some 900 feet above the floor of Paradise Valley, one comes to a tin mail box with the name "Goldwater" on it. Beyond the mailbox is a low, long, modernistic house, built in the shape of an arrow pointing toward Camelback Mountain, looming in the background.

The house itself is constructed of prehistoric pinkish red Arizona sandstone. Goldwater had discovered this distinctive stone on a Navajo Indian reservation during exploratory rambles in his youth, and had kept it in mind as the material for the house he would some day build. The long-deferred building day came in the late 1950's, and when it did, Goldwater had 200 tons of the strikingly colored sandstone shipped some 250 miles into Phoenix.

A $100,000 house was constructed from the sandstone. The doormat bears the name Be-Nun-I-Kin, which Goldwater explains is Navajo for House on the Top of the Hill. Green slate steps lead up to a gallery along one side of the house. The outer wall of the gallery is one huge picture window, looking out across the valley toward Phoenix; the inner wall is decorated with a display of Western paintings. Bedrooms open off the gallery. To the left of the gallery are the library, living room and kitchen. The right side of the gallery leads to a swimming pool, a two-room guest house, and a fish pond with water rippling down into it over rocks. Everywhere about the house and grounds are electronic gadgets.

Goldwater's personality is probably nowhere better expressed than in this fetish for gadgetry so evident in his home. He is an intensely physical and mechanically minded man. His sister, Carolyn, now Mrs. Bernard Erskine, once explained him in this quote: "I don't think he ever read a book growing up or missed an issue of Popular Mechanics." His home bears testament to his mechanical aptitude.

Take, for example, the electronic flagpole. Goldwater tinkered with this device for some time, finally got it to work. Now, when the sun rises, its beams activate an electric eye which in turn activates a motor which in turn raises the flag. When the sun sets, the first long shadows reverse the process, and the flag descends into a canister below the ground.

The electronic motif is everywhere. The headboard of Goldwater's bed looks almost like the instrument panel of a jet bomber. Controls regulate the outside lights, the air conditioning, the stereo hi-fi and the burglar alarm. But this is not all. Goldwater has installed a microphone beside the tiny waterfall that tumbles into his fish pond, and by this device he pipes the music of the rippling water to a loudspeaker beside his bed. He likes to go to sleep to the sound.

Gadgetry reaches its epitome in Goldwater's study. Here his built-in, diagonal desk reflects his interests. Within arm's reach are a two-way Unicom radio, an aircraft receiver, an anemometer to signal wind speed, a dictating machine, a short wave set. The push of a button unfurls a retractable movie screen.

Remarkable as are all these features of the Goldwater home, there is on the grounds a living presence more remarkable still. This is Goldwater's favorite brindle English bulldog named Cyclone. Cyclone is distinguished by a gold tooth. Almost as astonishing as the tooth itself is Goldwater's obvious pride in it. The columnist Jim Bishop reported: "On the Senator's shower door is a drawing of Cyclone's face, with the gold tooth hanging out of his mouth."

Such were the surroundings in which Barry Goldwater announced his candidacy. His decision to begin the race

with a patio-chat probably disenchanted no one more than
his attractive wife, Peggy. She had to get Maricopa County
sheriffs in their tight brown pants and dark brown 10-gallon
hats to fend off the curious. Since there wasn't room for
everyone, she had to throw open her living-room so that the
Arizona county chairmen could all gather there for a pre-
announcement announcement by Goldwater. Outside, she
had to watch while the television crews took over the garden,
while the carport was turned into a communications center
for telephone and Western Union lines. And, of course, she
had to provide tuna fish and cream cheese sandwiches and
coffee for the mob.

All such arrangements had been made, and the proceedings were about to start when Cyclone provided an unsched-
uled performance for the kickoff of the campaign. A neighborhood spaniel came snuffling inquisitively upon the scene,
and Cyclone, his gold tooth flashing, pitched into the in-
truder. It took about a dozen spectators to break up this
canine brawl so that the newsmen and television crews could
hear Goldwater pledge the Democrats a dogfight.

"I was once asked what kind of a Republican I was,"
Goldwater told his audience. "I replied that I was not a 'me-
too' Republican. That still holds. I will not change my beliefs
to win votes. I will offer a choice, not an echo. This will not
be an engagement of personalities. It will be an engagement
of principles."

Even in making this declaration, Goldwater was brought
into rather stark conflict with a principle he had once pro-
fessed. During the 1960 campaign, he had denounced Lyndon Johnson for practicing the rankest political trickery by
running for re-election to the U. S. Senate from Texas at
the same time that he was seeking the Vice Presidency. But
now, Goldwater said blandly, he intended to do the same
thing himself. Besides seeking the Presidential nomination,
he was going to file for re-nomination to the Senate. "I find
no incompatability in these two candidacies," he said.

He defined the issue of the 1964 campaign as one of "conscience" and "a definite choice."

"My candidacy is pledged to a victory for principle and to
presenting an opportunity for the American people to choose,"
he declared.

"Let there be a choice — right now and in clear, under-
standable terms."

Just two days later, on Sunday, January 5, Goldwater went

before a national television audience in a forum provided by *Meet the Press*. He was questioned about a number of the forthright and controversial stands he had taken during recent years. He had once advocated that the United States withdraw diplomatic recognition from Soviet Russia. Did he still favor such a course?

Yes, he did, Goldwater said. He explained that he would use the threat of withdrawal of recognition "as a bargaining effort to get some things accomplished." He thought optimistically that "the Soviet Union would do a lot to keep in our good graces" — things like maybe tearing down the Berlin wall or freeing the captive peoples of Eastern Europe — but then he added: "We have to keep in mind, though, this would take an action of the Senate of the United States. It is not just the whim of the President . . ."

Several times, Goldwater explained how essential Senate approval of such an action would be. The tragedy of it, of course, was that Goldwater, after serving nearly twelve years in the Senate, still had not learned that the Senate would not have to concur in breaking off diplomatic relations. The President, whose awesome powers he was seeking, has full authority in such cases; in fact, as the State Department pointed out afterward, President Roosevelt had granted Russia recognition in the thirties by a simple exchange of correspondence.

Next, Goldwater was asked about the nuclear test-ban treaty that the Kennedy administration had negotiated with Russia in the summer of 1963. Goldwater had fought against the treaty in the Senate and had voted against its ratification. What would he do about this issue if he were elected President?

"I would have to cross that bridge when I got to it," Goldwater said. "I still think it's of no advantage to the United States, and just the other day Dr. Hans Morgenthau, one of the great physicists of the world, backed up my position on that by stating what I said on the floor, that the treaty had more accrual of good to the Soviets than it did to the United States . . ."

One obvious flaw in this statement was that Dr. Morgenthau is not "one of the great physicists of the world." He is a professor of political science at the University of Chicago, eminent in his field and well-known as a writer. He had recently composed an article for *The New York Times Sunday Magazine* in which he had not supported Goldwater's position at all, but had cautioned against expecting too much from the test-ban treaty, warning that it did not automatically change the entire course and dialogue of the Cold War. Commenting on Goldwater's TV performance, Dr. Morgenthau groaned that Goldwater apparently had misunderstood his whole point.

Two such serious blunders in quick sequence would seem to constitute something of a record, but there was more to come. David Broder, of the *Washington Evening Star*, got the questioning into the sensitive civil rights territory. He pointed out that Goldwater had once said: "I would not like to see my party assume it is the role of the federal government to enforce integration in the schools." Was that still his attitude?

Goldwater could not recall ever having said any such thing. He added that if a federal court handed down an edict that a school district had violated the Supreme Court's ruling on integration, "I think it's incumbent on the federal government to enforce that edict."

Well, Broder wanted to know, did he disagree at all with the way Kennedy had handled the civil rights crises in the South? Would he, Goldwater, have used troops to uphold the law?

Goldwater squirmed. He conceded that Kennedy had probably had to act when the registration of Negro student James Meredith at the University of Mississippi had precipitated a full-scale and bloody riot. "I think, however, if you'll recall, he didn't use federal troops . . .," Goldwater said. "He sent federal marshals in. Now if an edict had been issued by a federal court, then I believe he has the right to use the federal marshals."

As a matter of historic fact — a fact that should have been remembered by any television-viewing schoolboy — President Kennedy in the Meredith case had sent in both regular Army troops and federalized National Guard troops when the rioting racist mobs threatened to overwhelm the small force of federal marshals who had first tried to cope with the situation.

There was more, but these were the classic goofs. Goldwater's performance was so startlingly inept, if not indeed revelatory of a fundamental ignorance about basic public issues, that even stalwart Republicans were horrified. Goldwater's friends, David Broder reported, saw such glaring slips as "an inattention to detail and an impreciseness of utterance" that could be disastrous in a campaign. One Republican leader went even further. "I keep thinking," he said about Goldwater, "that sometime he's going to be asked about a specific country, and he's not going to know whether it's in Asia or Africa. That could be embarrassing."

In the press, the reaction was equally shocked. Frank Coniff, columnist of the Hearst papers and a man hardly to be accused of any anti-Goldwater bias, wrote bluntly: "Sen. Goldwater's appearance on *Meet the Press* was a disaster." And Walter Lippmann, of the New York *Herald-Tribune*, long the sage of political commentators, was even more appalled. He wrote that Goldwater's insistence he could not, if President, sever relations with Russia "shows how little he understands the Constitutional powers of the office for which he is now an avowed candidate."

Lippman added:

"The essential Goldwater theme is the claim that he speaks the true and fundamental principles of the party of Washington and Hamilton, of Lincoln and Theodore Roosevelt, and of Eisenhower. To anyone brought up in a Republican tradition this is a preposterous claim. Senator Goldwater would transform the party of Hamilton into an anti-Federal party. He would transform the party of Lincoln into the party of the white supremacists. He would transform the party of Theodore Roosevelt into an anti-progressive party of uncontrolled and unregulated businessmen, each man for himself and the devil take the hindmost."

Barry Goldwater, Lippmann wrote, "is not a conservative at all. . . . He is a radical reactionary who would, if we are able to believe what he says, dismantle the modern state. His political philosophy does not have its roots in the conservative tradition but in the crude and primitive capitalism of the Manchester school. It is the philosophy not of the conservators of the social order but of the newly rich on the make."

CHAPTER III

Frontier Goldwaters

The Goldwater family were originally Polish Jews, and the name was spelled Goldwasser. Barry's great-grandfather was Hirsh Goldwasser who, with his wife, Elizabeth, ran an inn on a river bank in Konin, in the province of Poznan, then ruled by the Russia of the Czars. Hirsh and Elizabeth Goldwasser had a brood of twenty-two children, a flock that not only taxed the capacity of their inn but kept them in a constant struggle with penury.

One boy among the tribe seems to have stood out. He was tall, broad, muscular, good-looking, fair-haired. He was named Michel, or, as the name was later to be Anglicized, Michael. Quite early, he saw that all he could expect from life in Poland was drudgery for mere existence and almost certain impressment in the armies of the Czar. A Goldwater family tradition says that Michael rebelled at this fate, joined one of the innumerable and futile conspiracies the Poles were always concocting against Russian tyranny, was found out and had to flee for his life, hunted by the Czar's soldiers.

Only fifteen at the time, Michael made his way first into Germany and then on to Paris. He had been trained as a tailor, and he worked at this trade until the revolution of 1848 toppled the government of Louis Philippe. Uprooted by this development, Michael took his meager savings and fled to London. There he met a girl named Sarah Nathan, and in 1850 they were married.

The following year, Michael Goldwater was joined by a favorite brother from the brood he had left behind in Konin. This brother was named Joseph, and he was in almost every conceivable way the exact opposite of Michael. He was small in stature, swarthy and dark-haired. His left eyelid drooped, an affliction about which he was extremely sensitive and over which, bantam-like, he was prepared to do ferocious battle at the first facetious remark. Tall, handsome, easygoing and gregarious Michael; short, dark, dour and pugnacious Joe — they made a picture-book contrast; and in the rugged West of the old California Gold Rush days, they were almost instantly tabbed "Big Mike" and "Little Joe."

The California adventure, again according to family tradition, was probably undertaken at the instigation of Little Joe. He had been fascinated by the reports in Europe about the gold strike at Sutter's Mill, and his enthusiasm had been fired by intelligence he had gleaned from returning voyagers that there was no discrimination against Jews in America. Little Joe studied these two pieces of information, and he developed the idea that he and Big Mike should go to America, not to hunt gold themselves, but to get themselves a stake, invest in trade goods and do business with the miners in the gold camps.

Big Mike was reluctant to leave Sarah and the first two of their children (they were to have eight), but he was finally persuaded. And so in the spring of 1852 he and Little Joe sailed for California. They landed in San Francisco, and for two years they had to scrounge at any kind of job they could get to make a living. They finally collected a tiny nest egg and went on to Sonora, where gold was still being mined, intending to open a general store. The found, however, that Sonora already had several stores with which they could hardly hope to compete, and so they rented a location downstairs from a bordello and opened a saloon. This proved to be their first gold strike. Sex and liquor were always big commodities on the frontier; business flourished, and it wasn't long before Big Mike was able to send for Sarah and the children, Caroline and Morris. The latter was to have great influence on the future career of Barry Goldwater.

Sonora was a raw frontier town. Its law enforcement was primitive and often non-existent. Shootings, knifings and murders were the order of the day. Sarah Goldwater decided that it was no place to bring up children, and Big Mike was forced to agree with her. So he moved the family back to San Francisco, though he continued to operate the Sonora saloon while he looked around for a better business opportunity for himself and Little Joe.

He found it in Los Angeles, then just beginning to stir to life as a rival to San Francisco. A bar and billiard business in the Bella Union Hotel, just across the street from the present city hall, was up for sale, and Big Mike and Little Joe bought it. Once more they prospered. But Big Mike, whose traits seem to have been handed down in large measure to his famous grandson, had a restless, adventurous streak in him. He was never a man to be content to let well enough alone.

The last remaining real frontier was the Indian country in what was then called the New Mexico Territory. It lured Big Mike, and he set out with a wagon piled high with trade goods. Again he was successful, dealing with Indians and with the sparse settlers whose need for all kinds of goods was acute. Soon his expeditions into the wilds of the great Southwest were piling up sizable profits to be added to those of the Los Angeles bar and billiard business. Prospects looked rosy for the Goldwaters when disaster struck in the form of the depression of 1862. Money dried up, then vanished; the bar customers dried up and vanished, too; and things were looking grim when Mike heard about new placer gold strikes in the wild section along the Colorado River in what was soon to be named Arizona Territory.

A family council of war was held. The Goldwaters' savings had been almost wiped out; the once-flourishing Los Angeles bar was a losing proposition. If they continued as they were going, disaster was inevitable. They would have to strike out again in new endeavors. And so a decision was reached: Little Joe would go back to San Francisco seeking work and attempt to compile a new stake; Big Mike would try his luck in La Paz, Arizona; and once more Sarah and the children would wait until he could get enough money together to send for them.

This striking out for new frontiers again produced results. Big Mike went to work in La Paz in the store of a man named B. Cohen, a friend from Los Angeles; he soon became a partner in the business; and in 1867, when Cohen decided to sell out, Little Joe came on from San Francisco with the funds that made purchase of the business possible. So was founded the firm of M. Goldwater & Bro. — the foundation of all future Goldwater fortunes.

Within the next few years, the Goldwater brothers expanded their interests. Big Mike, ever adventurous, established a wagon hauling business, and he even laid out a new town on the Colorado not far from La Paz. He called it Ehrenberg in memory of a friend, Herman Ehrenberg, who had been killed by robbers. Here the Goldwaters located their principal store.

Life in the West in those days, however, was always a hazard. One bright spring morning in 1872, Big Mike and Little Joe hitched up their buggies for a trip from Prescott to Ehrenberg. On the way, passing through a narrow defile, they were jumped by a roving band of Apache-Mohaves. There were some thirty of the Indians, and they tore down out of the hills and along the road after Big Mike and Little Joe, firing their rifles as they came. The brothers lashed their horses in an effort to keep ahead. The chase lasted for several miles, bullets constantly winging past, and it began to look as if the brothers would almost certainly be surrounded and killed when, rounding a bend, they came upon a wagon train heading in the opposite direction. The plainsmen with the train quickly grabbed their rifles and began to fire at the Indians, who, having no stomach for this kind of opposition, turned and fled. Only then did Big Mike discover that his hat had a neat round hole in the crown — and, far worse, that Little Joe had two rifle balls in his back. The balls were extracted in a bit of crude frontier surgery, and Little Joe survived both the effects of the wounds and the treatment. Proud of his toughness, he had the slugs mounted on a watch fob that he carried for the rest of his life.

Such violence was never far beneath the surface of frontier life. It cropped out again on the Saturday night of December 8, 1883. Little Joe had opened a Goldwater store in Bisbee, and on this particular night he was arranging some merchandise on the shelves when he heard the door open and turned around to greet a customer. Instead, he found himself staring at three desperadoes, all with drawn guns pointed at him.

They demanded that Little Joe open the safe, and he was only too happy to oblige since he knew the money they wanted — the payroll of the Copper Queen Mine, which had been entrusted to him for safekeeping — wasn't in the safe, but was hidden in some sacks of barley at the rear of the store. Just as Little Joe opened the safe, however, a trigger-happy lookout posted outside the store shot a citizen who seemed to him too inquisitive. A second lookout began to fire, and the startled bandits, scooping what they could out of the safe, fled from the store, shooting as they went. By the time the fusillade was over, a young woman and three men had been killed.

A Sheriff's posse was organized in the best Wild West tradition, and after five days of hard riding, it tracked down the killers. When the prisoners were brought back, the citizens of Bisbee flew into lynch-minded rage. They were especially incensed against John Heath, one of the lookouts, a man who had operated a saloon across the street from the Goldwater store and who was believed to have cased the job for the robbers. As a result, on the night of February 22, 1884, a band of some fifty Bisbee citizens equipped themselves with a length of rope from Little Joe's stock, broke into the Tombstone jail, hustled Heath out and hanged him from the nearest tree. The robber gang were later hanged, too — legally.

In such a raw frontier atmosphere, the Goldwater businesses expanded. The territorial capital in the early days shifted back and forth between Prescott and Tucson before it finally located in Phoenix. During most of this period, Prescott had the call, and it was there that the Goldwaters established what was to be for years their major store.

All during these years of feverish activity on the part of Big Mike and Little Joe, Sarah Goldwater remained in California, separated for long periods from her husband. Sarah was a determined woman, and after her first shocking experience in Sonora, she had decided that her children were not going to be brought up in any frontier town; they were to have the advantages of city rearing and education. And so, except for the brief period when the Goldwaters were established in Los Angeles, Sarah kept the family home in San Francisco.

Baron Goldwater, the father of the future Senator and Presidential candidate, was born in Los Angeles, but spent all of his formative years in the city by the Golden Gate. He bore relatively little resemblance to his father. He was small and slender in stature and so fastidious in dress that he early acquired the reputation of being a dandy. But he had in marked degree one characteristic of Big Mike; he had a personality that charmed, a gift for making friends easily.

On October 31, 1882, when he was only sixteen years old, Baron Goldwater arrived in Prescott to begin his apprenticeship in the family enterprise. The Prescott store, which had been established by Big Mike, was then in the capable hands of Big Mike's first son, Morris, and another son, Henry. These older scions of the family, not unnaturally, exhibited a tendency to look down their noses at their "little brother," arriving from San Francisco garbed in dandified clothes purchased from Wanamaker's and exhibiting a penchant for using cologne. So Henry and Morris Goldwater gave Baron a job at the bottom of the ladder and left him to sink or swim.

Baron made no complaint. Whatever he was, he was not stupid, and so he worked hard, saved his money and studied the family business. His very upbringing, while it seemed to disqualify him for the ruggedness of frontier life, gave him a certain advantage of perspective over Morris and Henry. Baron could sense, as they could not, that the frontier was changing, that it was becoming slowly more civilized, and that its people would soon want some of the finer things of life. Testing this theory, Baron, on one of his trips to San Francisco, ordered a magnificent and expensive piano which he had shipped to Prescott. He sold it almost immediately at a handsome profit. Soon he was advertising pianos for sale as a regular Goldwater store item, and in a few months he disposed of more than a dozen. This success convinced Morris and Henry that "little brother" was every whit as smart as they were, and so, on Baron's twenty-eighth birthday, he was made a full partner in the business.

Henry, a roamer, adventurous like Big Mike, soon drifted out of the picture. Big Mike himself retired to California, where he was to settle down to a quiet domesticity for the last twenty years of his life. This left just Morris and Baron to take care of the family enterprises. Morris, a bachelor in his middle forties, was solidly established in Prescott. He was a Jeffersonian Democrat, the recognized leader of his party in the county, with an influence felt throughout the state. Prescott was not growing as fast as Phoenix, the new state capital, but Morris liked it and had no intention of moving. Opportunity called in Phoenix, however, and the Goldwaters felt they should have a store there. When they established it in 1896, Baron Goldwater went to Phoenix to head the new business.

He was immediately successful. He made regular buying trips to New York to purchase merchandise for both stores, and his taste in styles and materials was such that the Goldwater stores swiftly became noted for carrying goods of the best quality. As for Baron himself, he was quite a popular young man in Phoenix, good-looking, dressed to the nines, an engaging talker. Many a young lady set her cap for him, but Baron, it appeared, wasn't catchable. Like Morris, he seemed to prefer his bachelorhood.

Then, one day in 1903, a girl named Josephine Williams walked into the Goldwater store. She was a nurse from Illinois, and her father, Robert, claimed direct descent from pioneer Roger Williams, the founder of Rhode Island. Josephine was tall, blond, frail-looking, with a tell-tale flush to her cheeks. She had developed tuberculosis in Illinois and had been sent West for her health, which she quickly regained in the dry air of Arizona. Baron Goldwater found her appealing and attractive, and while he waited on her at the yard-goods counter, he tried out some of his best lines.

"I didn't buy what he tried to sell me," Josephine later told Stephen Shadegg, author of the official Goldwater biography. "It was too high-priced. But he was nice to talk to, although a little fresh and quite conceited."

The record would seem to indicate that Baron wasn't used to being snubbed, and so he set out in pursuit that lasted more than a year and had all the younger world of Phoenix quite agog. Finally, Josephine capitulated. When they became engaged, Baron was 41 and she was 29.

"I wasn't the prettiest girl in town by a long shot," Josephine told Shadegg long years later. "I wasn't the youngest or the wealthiest; in fact, I think Baron regarded me as a hard case because I didn't faint at his flattery."

There can be no question that Josephine Williams possessed a sturdy and independent spirit. A graphic illustration of this may be seen in her decision about her wedding dress. Baron suggested she could have the pick of the dresses in the Goldwater store. Indignantly, she refused. Until she was married, she told him, she would buy her own clothes and pay for them, and so she bought some yard goods, at another store, and had a seamstress fashion her wedding dress.

"It was a pretty dress, but not as nice as the ones he had in the store," Josephine later told Shadegg. "He knew it and I knew it, but we never said anything. He respected my independence and all our life together we were that way."

The newlyweds set up housekeeping in a large, rented, two-story house at 710 North Central Avenue, the site of the present Westward Ho Hotel, and it was here, on New Year's Day, 1909, that Barry Morris Goldwater was born.

CHAPTER IV

The Young Barry

The Phoenix of Barry Goldwater's boyhood was more frontier village than modern city. Where today Phoenix houses more than 500,000 citizens, there were then barely 10,000. The streets were unpaved and filled with choking dust in the hot summers. Horses pulling buggies were only rarely frightened by the chugging of an occasional automobile. Open ditches bordered the roads, filtering water to trees that had been planted by some of the founders. There were, of course, no sidewalks, and cottonwoods cast their shadow over what were to be some of the principal avenues of the future metropolis.

There were soon three children in the Goldwater family, a brother, Bob, who was 18 months younger than Barry, and a sister, Carolyn. From their earliest days, there was one paramount influence on their lives — that of their mother, Josephine, whom Barry as a child called "Mun," a nickname that stuck. Never were parents more opposite in their traits, and never did a son grow to be more unlike his father.

Baron Goldwater, marrying late after a long bachelorhood, accommodated himself to married life readily enough. He took great pride in Josephine, whose verve and wit soon sparked much of the social life of Phoenix. But adjusting to his own children was another matter. Baron Goldwater evidently never felt quite at home with his offspring, nor they with him. When he came home from the store, he liked the house quiet, and Josephine tried to put a damper on the children's high spirits and keep it that way. Inevitably, the act put a certain distance between Baron and the children themselves. In later life, Barry Goldwater was to comment that, while he always felt certain Baron loved them all very deeply, he had never been able to feel really close to his father.

Baron's personality, too, set him apart. Throughout his life, he remained extremely fastidious. He would often come home in the afternoon to wash and put on a clean shirt. He never soiled his hands with physical labor if he could get someone else to do it. He was so helpless mechanically, this man whose oldest son was to feel most at home in the world of mechanics, that he could not fix a leaky faucet. He never even learned to drive a car.

Josephine was all the things that Baron was not. She had the hardy traits of a pioneer woman. As a tiny girl back in Illinois, she had trailed along after her older brothers on camping and hunting trips. She was as familiar with a shotgun as any man — and was a dead shot with a rifle. After she was married, she liked to go out in the desert, hunting for rabbits, snakes, anything that offered a moving target. One Goldwater family legend has it that, one day after the Goldwaters had obtained a car, Baron went for a ride with Josephine out into the desert. She was doing the driving, of course, and she had her rifle with her. Baron, squinting, scanning the horizon, saw something moving far ahead. It was a roadrunner (or chaparral cock).

Pointing out the target to Jo, he said:

"Let's see you hit that, sharpshooter."

Accepting the challenge, Jo whipped the rifle to her shoulder, sighted, fired. The roadrunner flipped high into the air and dropped dead. Baron never questioned his wife's marksmanship again.

In such a family, it is easy to see who would be the mentor of the children. Josephine Goldwater's traits became inevitably those that set the family standards, those that have endured.

One of these traits was a fervent patriotism. This found expression in a symbolic act. When the children were all quite small, Josephine used to take them almost every evening to the U. S. Government Indian School about two and a half miles from their home. In dust and burning heat, they would all walk the distance, Jo and the nurse taking turns carrying Carolyn in their arms, the boys trudging along beside them. They would arrive at the school shortly before sunset, and there the boys would stand at attention during the performance they had come to witness — the playing of the Star Spangled Banner and the lowering of the flag.

In summer, Jo led the family on camping expeditions. Everyone who could fled the suffocating heat of Phoenix.

Baron, of course, had to stay behind to mind the store, but Jo would take the children on long rambles in the northern Arizona mountains or on a five-day drive across desert and mountains to the Southern California seashore. Summer, as a result, was always a time of exploration and adventure, and Barry Goldwater, when he was only five, learned from his mother how to make camp, cut wood and start a fire.

Such were the formative influences of Barry Goldwater's life. These experiences of the boy show in the activities and philosophy of the man.

From the start, Barry was in many respects a problem child, a little hell-raiser. He was a bundle of physical activity, adventurous, combative, an incorrigible prankster. His parents became concerned because there was a time when he seemed to get into a new fight every day. And some of his pranks seemed to go beyond mere pranks and reveal a streak of cruelty.

In this category was a penchant he developed for purloining his friends' bicycles and hiding them to make the owners believe they had been stolen and irrevocably lost. Barry seemed to take a delight in his victims' tears. On one occasion, he went further. He pilfered the bicycle of Ray Johnson (who was to become a vice-president of the New York Life Insurance Co.), dismantled it, and hid the parts in his attic. It took an angry personal call by Johnson's father at the Goldwater home to recover the vehicle.

During the World War I years of 1917 and 1918, the boys of Phoenix simulated the trench warfare of the Western Front in their games. They dug trenches and pelted each other with mud balls. Barry Goldwater was one of the leaders of the North Central Gang in their warfare with the First Street Gang, and he is credited with changing the tactics of the game. At his instigation, the North Centrals began to encase rocks in their mud balls.

All such escapades paled, however, before one Fourth of July prank of Barry's. He was nine at the time. In those days, air conditioning had not yet been invented, and from late spring on, virtually the entire population of Phoenix slept outdoors, seeking relief from the heat. The Goldwaters had a large screened-in porch that extended across the back of their North Central Avenue home, and it was here that the entire family slept. Barry had noticed that his mother, true to her frontier instincts, always kept a loaded revolver under her pillow, and it occurred to him that this would be better than any firecracker to celebrate the Fourth.

So, after everyone else had gone to sleep, Barry stole to his mother's bedside, carefully extracted the revolver without disturbing her, pointed it at the porch roof and blazed away. The barrage jolted the entire neighborhood. Barry's father jumped out of bed and stared unbelievingly at his nine-year-old son holding a smoking revolver in his hand, and Jo had to explain to neighbors that it was nothing really — just Barry prematurely celebrating the Fourth of July. The incident might have passed without further notice, except for one thing. Barry's father had stored two kegs of home brew in a room on the second floor, acting on the theory that the heat there would speed the fermentation of the whisky — and one of the errant bullets plugged a keg. When the porch ceiling began to drip whisky, Baron Goldwater flew into one of his rare furies, and, as Barry said years later, "I caught it something fierce."

The prankish streak in Barry Goldwater was aided and abetted by his strong mechanical bent. His mother subscribed to *Popular Mechanics* and a number of other scientific and technical magazines. Barry devoured this fare avidly, the one type of literature for which he showed any affinity. There is a Goldwater family legend that his mother tried to introduce him to Gibbons' *Decline and Fall of the Roman Empire* when he was only eight. Neither this nor other books with which he was later thrown into contact seem to have made much impression on Barry, but it was different with the diagrams and designs in the mechanical journals. These fascinated him, and soon he was busily endeavoring to follow the directions and build the devices.

He constructed model airplanes, built a crystal radio set, took up photography. The new medium of radio especially fascinated him. He began to hang around Earl Neilson's radio shop in Phoenix, sweeping the floors and washing windows in return for instruction, and by the time he was 12, he was skillful enough to help Neilson and others construct the first commercial radio transmitter in the town — station KFAD. He acquired one of the first amateur radio licenses in Phoenix and claims to have been the city's first disc jockey, playing records over the air. This interest, so early developed, endures to this day and is reflected in the ham radio stations he maintains in his Phoenix home and Washington apartment.

This love of mechanics, this fascination with gadgetry of all kinds, reinforced and gave new outlets to the practical-prankster's side of his nature. He delighted in snapping candid camera shots of persons in unflattering and embarrassing positions. He took impish delight in rigging the bathroom of the Goldwater home for sound. By means of a microphone and a loudspeaker, he could communicate with anyone who happened to be enjoying the privacy of the bathroom, and many a female guest of the Goldwaters was startled by hearing a masculine voice suddenly say familiarly, almost in her ear, "Hi, there, honey — what's new?"

An indication that this strain runs deep in Goldwater may be seen in the fact that he did not soon outgrow it. Years later, during the 1940 Western Amateur golf tournament, held in Phoenix, Barry concealed a loudspeaker under the hole on the 18th green and ran a wire underground to a hidden microphone. As each golfer finished his round and reached into the cup for his golf ball, he was startled to hear a mysterious voice booming comments up to him from the very ground. It was a panic. Goldwater and the gallery loved it.

During the prankrish boyhood days in Phoenix, one of Barry's best friends was Harry Rosenzweig, who was eighteen months his senior. Rosenzweig, who was to become a prominent Phoenix jeweler and to remain a life-long friend, lived in a house just two blocks away, and the two boys became inseparable. They established what they called the North Central Avenue Athletic Club and held meetings and contests in a large room over the huge garage at the back of the Goldwater home. Baron Goldwater, although he shunned physical activity himself, encouraged the boys' athletic bent, and whenever he made buying trips to New York, he would ship home some new kind of gym equipment. The boys set up a ring and charged twenty-five cents admission to their boxing bouts. Their instructor was a neighborhood Negro whom they called "Old Grey Dad" and whose son became one of their sparring partners. The son was John Henry Lewis, later light-heavyweight champion of the world.

In all such physical and mechanical activities, Barry Goldwater excelled. He and Bob took up swimming, and in one meet at Tempe Beach they brought home fourteen ribbons between them. Bob, though a good athlete, was not outstanding as was Barry. On the other hand, he was mentally much the keener of the two. While Barry struggled for passing grades in grammar school, Bob skipped two half-years' work, and by the time the boys entered the seventh grade, he had caught up to Barry. Indeed, at times, he was doing much of Barry's homework. In the fall of 1923, the brothers were ready for high school, and they enrolled together at Phoenix Union, then the only public high school in the Arizona capital.

The school had a larger campus and enrollment than many a western state college, and its athletic teams often played and defeated teams in the lower collegiate ranks. The young Barry Goldwater, a personality kid from his very toes, hit Phoenix Union with the impact of a bombshell. He was promptly elected president of his freshman class. He played freshman football and basketball, and he was to his classmates quite the big shot, quite the hero. There was just one trouble — his studies. He flunked two courses outright and barely squeaked by in the others.

School officials conferred solicitously with the Goldwaters, who were just about the most prominent family in Phoenix. "They told us," Josephine said years afterward, "that maybe Barry should become a priest, because the only thing he was good at was Latin."

A less likely candidate for the priesthood could hardly be imagined. Josephine and Baron Goldwater, alarmed by their son's appalling marks, sat down and consulted about what they should do. They decided that they had been too indulgent with Barry, that what he needed was a strong taste of military discipline. And so they decided to send their problem son to the Staunton Military Academy in Virginia. It turned out to be a wise choice.

Discipline at the academy was tough, and Staunton had a hazing system for new cadets that rivaled anything West Point could offer. Barry Goldwater, so recently the big shot of the freshman class at Phoenix Union, found himself relegated to the menial category of flunky to an upper classman. He had to polish his master's shoes, make his master's bed, clean and shine his rifle — and he had to do it all correctly, and without a murmur of protest. The comedown must have been a shock for young Barry, but it says much about his inner core of toughness that he liked it and thrived upon it. Tough demands were a challenge, and he always liked to meet and whip a challenge. So began a love affair with the military that was to last all his life.

Barry had to repeat his freshman year's classes at Staunton, and so he was there for a full four years. "His poor marks and undisciplined nature" sometimes "made the faculty wish he had never come there," one account of these years says. But this was just one side of the picture. On the athletic field, on the drill field, Barry was a leader. He broke his nose playing center on the football team. He hurled the javelin in track and captained the swimming team. In his senior year, he commanded the top cadet company and won the coveted Kable Medal as the outstanding all-around cadet.

These triumphs behind him, Barry Goldwater returned to Phoenix in the fall of 1928 and prepared for college. He acquired a 1925 Chrysler roadster, and he enrolled in the freshman class of the University of Arizona in Tucson. He had just one purpose in mind, as he later confessed — to have himself a ball. Sigma Chi fraternity had pledged his brother Bob at the University of Illinois the year before, and Barry was determined to make Sigma Chi at Arizona. He did. Six feet tall and weighing 185 pounds, he went out for freshman football and promptly became the anchor man in the center of the freshman line. He was so good that the varsity coach, impressed by his speed, agility and aggressiveness, began to see him as next year's No. 1 varsity center.

The pattern was recognizable. It was recognizable, too, in other ways. Barry Goldwater was quite the campus social lion in his class, but studies bored him just as much as they always had. His Chrysler roadster was to be seen most often parked in front of the Pi Phi or the Theta sorority house. He served as chairman of the Freshman Stadium Fund Committee, participating energetically in the drive to raise funds to build a new varsity stadium, and he was elected president of his class for the second semester. But he remained indifferent to any intellectual challenge, and a bare C average was the best he could amass.

It was a gay ball while it lasted, but it all ended for Barry Goldwater with a crash on the evening of March 6, 1929. That evening, an urgent telephone call came for Barry at the Sigma Chi house. He was out on the town as usual, and his fraternity brothers fanned out across the campus looking for him.

In Phoenix, the time that catches up to all men had caught up with Baron Goldwater at the age of 63. He had been suffering for years from angina pectoris, a heart disease, but he had insisted to his doctor that no one in the family was to know. He had lived with his lonely pain and his lonely sentence, and not even Jo had been aware of his ailment. But on this day, acting on some inexplicable premonition, she had broken off a golf match she was winning in a tournament, and hurried home. She had found Baron in bed, stricken by a pain worse than any he had previously endured. Before a doctor could arrive from only a few blocks away, Baron Goldwater clutched Jo's hand hard one last time, gasped and died.

Barry and Bob hurried home for the funeral. After it was over, they sat down to discuss the future.

"One of us should get a college education," Barry said, "and it had better be you. I'll come back and start learning something about the store."

CHAPTER V

Merchant Prince

When 20-year-old Barry Goldwater returned to Phoenix to take up his life's career, he found the most fascinating challenges facing him on every side. "Learning something about the store" was, of course, the principal one; but it was by no means alone. There was the wonder and mystery of Arizona, its vastness still not completely explored. There was the challenge of learning to fly. And, of course, inevitably, there was the challenge of pretty girls.

Barry Goldwater threw himself with headlong zest into the effort to meet and sample all of these challenges. When his father died, the store was left in the capable hands of Sam Wilson, its general manager, a veteran who had worked for the firm ever since 1909. Wilson and Josephine Goldwater decided between them that, if Barry was to become a merchant prince, he had better learn the hard way — from the bottom up.

So the social lion of Arizona U. went to work in Goldwater's as a clerk at $20 a week. He swept floors, counted stock, measured yardgoods and made deliveries just like any other $20-a-week clerk, and it wasn't long before he demonstrated, as had his father before him, that he had a special aptitude for the life.

All sources agree that Barry Goldwater was a champion salesman. He had in abundant quantity the salesman's indispensable asset, personal charm. One of the first acts of Sam Wilson was to station him in the piece goods department. Barry quickly studied and learned everything that he could about piece goods, the quality of cloth, the various patterns, the different uses of material — and then he turned on the charm. Almost before Sam Wilson knew what was happening, it seemed that every female in Phoenix was flocking to the piece goods counter to be waited on by handsome young Barry Goldwater.

"We don't even sell piece goods now," Bob Goldwater later told Rod Wood and Dean Smith, who wrote an admiring biography of Goldwater. "But Barry made it a hot item during his early years with the store. He was — and still is — a terrific salesman."

Proof may be found in some of the sales records in which Barry Goldwater still takes pride. Transferred to the ready-to-wear department, he set a store record one Christmas season by racking up 204 sales in a single day. The second year he was with the store he set an all-time record for individual sales. Years later, when a political opponent referred to him scathingly as "a ribbon clerk," Goldwater retorted that it was right, he had been — and "a damn good ribbon clerk," too.

No selling of piece goods, no setting of records in ready-to-wear, could gratify Barry Goldwater's insatiable zest for life or drain his abundant energy. Even today, he operates on a full head of steam with only five hours sleep, and in his twenties, sleep was the last of his worries. There was so much to do.

He was living at the time with his mother (Bob and Carolyn were both away at school) in the large house on North Central. Deciding he wanted to learn to fly but not wanting to worry his mother, he would get up at 5 A.M., sneak quietly out of the house, drive to the airport and get in an hour's flying instruction before he had to report for work in the store. His quiet departures, of course, did not long escape the notice of Josephine. She knew her son was up to something ("I think she thought I was chasing some babe," Barry has said), but she didn't know what it was until she read an item in the local newspaper that Barry Goldwater had obtained his private pilot's license.

Flying and hard work in the store did not fill all Barry Goldwater's hours. He still had time for some typical hi-jinks. One Saturday night he and two friends, Paul Morris and A. J. Bayless, later the proprietor of a large chain of Arizona supermarkets, set out on a 200-mile drive to Nogales, Sonora, just across the Mexican border from Nogales, Arizona. Prohibition had laid its clammy hand on America, but Nogales, Sonora, was a wide-open fun town. After driving all night, Goldwater and his friends reached their destination shortly after daybreak and decided to have breakfast at a sidewalk cafe.

They had just started to eat when, one thing leading to another, Paul Morris tossed a beaker of beer at Barry. Grabbing the nearest object, a mustard pot, Barry hurled it at Morris. Unfortunately, his aim was bad. The mustard pot sailed past its intended target and splattered its contents all over the uniform of a policeman standing nearby.

There was, as they say, the very hell to pay. Morris and Bayless managed to flee back across the border, but Barry was hustled to the local pokey and put behind bars. Word of his plight quickly got around, and old college friends in Nogales, Arizona, crossed the border, asking permission to see Barry Goldwater. When shown the prisoner, they would look Barry straight in the eye, shake their heads and solemnly assure the police that this man was not Barry Goldwater. It was funny at first, but Goldwater could soon see that his friends were placing him in a nice spot. How was he ever going to convince the Mexican police of his identity? How was he ever going to get out of that Mexican jail?

Barry decided the time had come to tackle the problem. He demanded to see the police chief. The chief informed him he had been fined $50 and he could not be released until the fine had been paid. Could he pay by check, Barry wondered. Possibly, the chief said, but he would have to be assured the check was good; he would have to know just who his young American prisoner was. Barry decided the time had come for confession. Pretending that he was at last making a clean breast of everything, he told the chief that his real name was A. J. Bayless; he was the son of the prominent Phoenix grocer, J. B. Bayless. Perhaps the chief had heard of Bayless? He had. Well, said Barry, he had not acknowledged his true identity immediately because he had not wanted to embarrass his family.

The chief could understand such a sensitive and honorable impulse. He obtained a blank check, and Barry filled it in and signed with a flourish the name, A. J. Bayless. The chief accepted the check, and Barry, freed from jail, returned to Phoenix.

"He said they never would have let him out if he hadn't mentioned my name," Bayless told Shadegg, chuckling about the incident years later, "and he told Paul to remember any time he got in trouble in Nogales, Sonora, just to call the chief of police and mention the name, A. J. Bayless."

Bayless didn't know what it was all about until the check was presented for payment, and a clerk in the Phoenix bank questioned the signature. Then came the revelation, and Bayless understood why Barry Goldwater had looked so pleased with himself when he came back across the border. Deciding the laugh was on him, Bayless told the bank to honor the check.

Such escapades, added to Barry's childhood record of being a little terror, had given him quite a distinctive reputation in Phoenix by the time Margaret (Peggy) Johnson arrived on the scene. Peggy was petite and beautiful, with pretty brown hair, deep blue eyes and a gorgeous complexion. Her father, Ray Prescott Johnson, of Muncie, Indiana, had been for many years president of the Warner Gear Company, and he was one of the founders, through the amalgamation of several firms, of the multi-million-dollar Borg-Warner Corporation, one of the nation's largest makers of auto accessories and equipment.

The Johnsons had begun going to Phoenix to spend the winters in 1929. Peggy, an art student, was in school in the East at the time. After attending Mount Vernon seminary in Washington, she studied at the Grand Central Art School in New York and later went into fashion designing, working for the David Crystal Company, one of New York's major dress manufacturing firms. On visits to her family in Phoenix, she had heard much about the rambunctious Goldwater family, but she had not met any of them until she went into the Goldwater store with her mother to do some pre-Christmas shopping. There, in the same surroundings in which nurse Josephine Williams had met Baron Goldwater, Peggy's mother introduced her to young Barry.

Peggy was impressed. Handsome six-foot Barry, with his dark curly hair, his energy, his flashing smile and warm personality, registered instantly with Peggy Johnson.

"I decided to find out more about him," she has said. "The first thing I found out was that the competition for his attentions was terrific."

Barry Goldwater, like his father before him, was just about the most eligible young bachelor in Phoenix, and he was playing the field with the greatest of relish. Peggy Johnson herself was at no loss for admirers. One of her steadiest escorts of the period — a fact that was to be much noted later — was a young man named G. Mennen Williams, who was to become Governor of Michigan and a liberal Democrat whose political philosophy was at the opposite pole from the ultra-conservative creed of Barry Goldwater.

Romance rather than politics was the preoccupation of the moment, however, and Peggy Johnson and Barry Goldwater, after their first casual meeting, went their separate ways. In January, 1932, Peggy's father suffered a stroke, and she gave up her job in New York to go to Phoenix to be with him. The Johnsons, for a time, occupied an apartment next to the Goldwaters' North Central Avenue home. There Peggy nursed her father for months, and he seemed on the road to recovery. But in November, 1932, he suffered a second stroke and died.

It was during this period that Barry Goldwater began to take more notice of the pretty girl next door. Before Peggy and her mother, Ann, left Phoenix that winter, they gave a party for their local friends. The Goldwaters were invited, and Barry took a longer and closer look at the pretty, dark-haired girl from Muncie. He evidently liked what he saw; for that summer, when Peggy and her mother went to the Johnson family place at Charlevoix, Michigan, who should appear upon the scene, entirely by accident, of course, but Barry Goldwater.

He came for a weekend and stayed two weeks. Before he left, he was proposing to Peggy, but she put him off, saying she was not ready for marriage yet. No such excuse could deter Barry Goldwater. The remaining months of 1933 were filled with the activity of his persistent courtship. He wrote, he phoned, he chased in person whenever he could get the opportunity. The Christmas season, though the busiest period of the year in the store, found him in Muncie dancing attendance on Peggy.

The climax to his cross-country wooing came one New Year's Eve. Peggy and Barry went to a New Year's Eve dance. Throughout the evening, he kept proposing; she kept putting him off. Midnight came, a cannon boomed, and the new year of 1934 was upon them. Peggy went to a phone booth to call her mother with New Year's wishes. Barry went with her, penned her in the booth, and demanded an answer. He has related the incident many times since in approximately these words:

"I told her, 'Look, I love you, but I can't keep this up. I have a business to run. It's got to be yes or no — right now.'"

Faced with this ultimatum, Peggy gave her answer — "Yes." An elated Barry Goldwater rushed back to Phoenix and airmailed her an engagement ring. He wanted an early wedding, but Peggy delayed. She had promised her mother to go with her on a world cruise in the spring, and she felt that they should go through with their plans. Barry protested, but in vain. So he did the next best thing. He wrote reams of letters, sent presents. At every port of call, there were mementos waiting for Peggy.

Back in the States by late summer, Peggy began to make preparations for her wedding. Since Barry Goldwater, though his father's line was Jewish, had been reared in the Episcopal faith by his mother, Peggy Johnson joined the Episcopal Church, and on September 22, 1934 she and Barry were wed in the Grace Episcopal Church in Muncie.

The first years of marriage were happy and hectic. The depression, which began in the East with the stock market collapse of 1929, spread slowly like a wasting disease across the land. Its full effects were not felt in Phoenix until the early thirties, but then they were so devastating that Goldwater himself has said it was for a time "touch and go" whether the store could meet its payroll, whether it could survive. Cheaper lines of merchandise were added to the usual high-quality, high-priced Goldwater stock; salaries and costs were cut; and though other merchandisers were forced to close their doors, Goldwater's weathered the storm. And — a matter of pride with Goldwater — it did so without firing a single employee.

During the mid-1930's Barry assumed full control of the business. He soon attracted national attention with his novel ideas. One of these was for "Antsy Pantsy" shorts. Goldwater's mind played around with the expression, "You've got ants in your pants," and he began to wonder what would happen if he turned saying into reality. Acting on the impulse, he had a white cotton fabric designed with huge red ants crawling all over it. Then he had the material made into underwear for men. For months, the store had difficulty keeping up with orders from all over the nation.

A second coup of Goldwater's stemmed from one of his innumerable hobbies. He had become a fascinated collector of western branding irons, and it occurred to him that the branding iron motif, transferred to fabrics, might do as much for women's blouses and mens sports shirts as the ants had for the pants. Soon Goldwater's was selling even window draperies with the branding iron design printed on them. The Arizona demand was tremendous, and Goldwater decided to promote his idea by advertising in the *New Yorker* magazine. It was the first national advertising ever done by an Arizona department store, and a flood of orders descended upon Goldwater's from every state in the nation.

The work and strain of this period became too much for Goldwater and led to a couple of crackups that are almost certain to become political ammunition in the 1964 campaign. Though the Rob Wood-Dean Smith biography contained a passing reference to the events, not much attention had been paid to them until an article about Peggy Goldwater, entitled, "The Woman Behind Barry Goldwater," appeared in the May, 1964 issue of *Good Housekeeping.* The article, written by Washington free-lancer Alvin Toffler, discussed some of the trials of the Goldwaters' lives in these terms:

"One crisis occurred in 1937 when, after a period of intense work in the store, Barry suffered a nervous breakdown. After a lengthy rest, he went back to work. But two years later, when he went to Prescott, Arizona, to help open a new branch of the store, and spent five days and nights without sleep, he cracked up again. 'His nerves broke completely,' says Mrs. Goldwater. 'He couldn't sleep nights. He was very nervous. I immediately said we were going to get away to Honolulu. He was seasick all the way. But then he relaxed on the beach and just rested.' The change of pace was, apparently, all he needed."

Wood and Smith, who had obtained a virtually identical version from the Goldwater family for their earlier biography, concluded their account this way: "Doctors warned him that his life might be a short one if he didn't learn to relax. Barry tried taking cat naps. He learned to hold his temper in check. He has had no trouble with nervous tension since."

When *Good Housekeeping* called attention to the two nervous breakdowns, there, almost instantly, was all kinds of trouble. Drew Pearson, the nationally syndicated columnist, hopped on the disclosure, and newspapers across the nation took notice. The emerging theme seemed to be: Granted that the pressures of running a large department store are severe, they are not to be compared to the crushing tensions of the Presidency. If Barry Goldwater, in his late twenties, had cracked under the department store strain, what might he do in his mid-fifties if he had to shoulder the awesome burdens of the office he was seeking?

Such speculation, understandably, angered the Goldwaters. In California, Barry's 25-year-old son, Barry Goldwater Jr., told the San Francisco *Chronicle* angrily:

"That's hogwash. My father did have one breakdown when he was 26 years old. But he had been working too hard and it was strictly physical. It was not mental."

The evidence seems to show that Barry Goldwater, a nice guy personally, could be something of a terror as an executive. Wood and Smith say that, as a boss, he "was both a joy and a trial to his secretaries. He could be a roaring volcano, ranting and swearing when faced with a trying situation, and within the hour perform some act of kindness that his subordinates never forgot."

The Goldwater volcano threw off sparks in many directions. Hard as he might work in the store, Barry Goldwater played just as hard, if not harder, at his hobbies. From boyhood he had been fascinated by the Indians of Arizona, by the mysteries of the great Grand Canyon, and in adult life he studied and explored both. In 1937 he and Peggy traveled 1,200 miles through the lands of the Navajos without once following an established road. Everywhere he went in Indian country, Barry Goldwater, the boyhood camera enthusiast, shot innumerable pictures to record the life he saw. He finally amassed some 8,000 photographs of twelve Indian tribes and the remote scenic splendors of Arizona, and the best of these he reproduced in 1940 in a two-volume work called *Arizona Portraits.* The excellence of his photography was such that the Royal Photographer's Society of London granted him an associate membership.

Roaming the Indian reservations, Goldwater became fascinated by the Kochina dolls of the Hopis. These are small, masked figures carved by Indian fathers from cottonwood roots and stained with vegetable dyes made by chewing leaves and roots and spitting the colored juice through the teeth. Kochinas are presented to children by their parents to teach them about the supernatural creatures the Hopis worship. Goldwater, as the result of years of persistent collecting on Indian reservations, has acquired a collection of some 350 Kochinas. It is insured for some $35,000.

Goldwater's interest in Indian lore is matched by his enthusiasm for the natural wonders of Arizona. As a boy of ten, he rode a donkey down the difficult Grand Canyon trails, and the Canyon and the mighty Colorado River that roars through its gorge have always fascinated him. For years, Goldwater was possessed by a fever he describes as "riveritis," and in 1940 he joined an expedition for the perilous adventure of shooting the rapids of the Green and Colorado Rivers by boat. The turbulent waters dashed one of the boats in the expedition to pieces against the rocks, and Goldwater's craft, spun and tossed in the wild water, was forced so low that Goldwater later wisecracked, "I swear there was gravel in my hair from the bottom of the river when I finally emerged." Six times in subsequent years

Goldwater has challenged the rapids of the Colorado, and six times he has won. He has recorded many of his experiences on film, and the pictures and brief accompanying text describing his first extended trip resulted in another book, *An Odyssey of the Green and Colorado Rivers*, published in 1941.

Not by boat and trail alone, however, has Goldwater been content to explore the landscape of his native state. In 1951, flitting in his private plane about the vast and still not fully explored reaches of the canyon country, he spotted the shadow of a previously undiscovered natural bridge falling across the wall of Nankoweap Canyon. Possessed by the thrill of discovery, Goldwater landed at the nearest airport, rented a helicopter and had the pilot land him near the bridge. Treacherous winds sweeping the gorge buffeted the helicopter, and the pilot had to take off, leaving Goldwater alone in the heart of the desolate terrain. This did not bother Goldwater. He spent hours photographing his discovery from every possible angle; then he climbed some 2,000 feet to the rim of the canyon and safety. The bridge he had discovered he named Margaret Arch, in honor of Peggy.

Such was the man, such the life of the Goldwaters in the early years of their marriage. They had four children — Joanne, Barry Jr., Michael and Peggy — and the life they led was the comfortable and pleasant one associated with the rich executive class. The routine was enlivened by buying trips to New York City for the store; by vacations in Acapulco and Mexico City and Nassau; and by rambles and explorations in Arizona's canyon and Indian country. Peggy Goldwater makes no secret of the fact that she wishes this time of their lives could have lasted forever.

"Life was so simple," she has said.

It was not to remain that way for much longer.

CHAPTER VI

War and Politics

War clouds thickened, and Barry Goldwater itched to get into the conflict.

By the spring of 1941, it had become clear to many that the sweep of Hitler's Nazi legions over most of Western Europe menaced the lives of free men everywhere and that, only by the greatest of good fortune, could the United States avoid being dragged into the holocaust that was forever expanding and devastating new areas of the world.

Barry Goldwater, with the martial outlook and enthusiasm he had imbibed at Staunton, was convinced that America would have to fight; and, characteristically, he was determined to get into the thick of the action. His love of flying combined with his thirst for danger and adventure set his goal. He wanted a commission in the Air Corps.

This seemed like the most fanciful of ambitions, impossible of fulfillment. Barry Goldwater was 32, married, the father of four children. He had stiff and creaky knees, the result of injuries sustained on the basketball court in his youth. And he was afflicted with astigmatism that prevented him from passing the Air Corps' rigid eyesight examinations. These various and obvious disqualifications might have daunted a less determined man — but not Barry Goldwater.

He pounded on the doors of recruiting officers. Turned down with pitying smiles, he appealed for help to Arizona's United States Senators, the veteran Carl Hayden and Ernest W. McFarland, a man whom, ironically, in just a few short years, Goldwater was to retire from politics. Hayden and McFarland helped, and Goldwater, with their assistance, made an end run to his objective.

He had earned a reserve commission during his four years at Staunton, and he had kept it in force ever since by attending periodic training drills. On the basis of this commission, he applied for active duty with the Army, as an officer attached to the Air Corps at Luke Field, Arizona. To qualify physically, he had to undergo an operation on his battered knees, to remove damaged cartilage; and, thus restored to mobility, he was accepted for active duty in September, 1941. He was commissioned a first lieutenant and was made a gunnery instructor in the training command.

This was only the first step for Goldwater. He still wanted his wings, and he soon figured out a way to get flight training on the sly. Goldwater began taking his camera aloft with him when he rode in the rear cockpit of training planes. He would photograph the pilots of other planes as they flew past, and he would give the pilots these graphic in-action shots to send back to their sweethearts and their families. Naturally, the pilots were grateful, and naturally they were glad to recompense the charming Barry Goldwater in the only coin he wanted — a chance to take over the controls of their planes when they were aloft and no one was looking.

A natural flier, Goldwater soon got the feel of training planes, and almost before the Air Corps realized what had happened, or how, he applied for a flight check, passed it and received a limited flight rating. More flying, more training followed, and ultimately Barry Goldwater achieved his ambition — he obtained the coveted wings of a full-fledged military pilot.

Though too old for combat, he was eligible for the ferry command service. In May, 1943, he joined the ferry command at Wilmington, Del., and soon he was flying the new P-47 fighters across the Atlantic to England for service on the Western Front. His success on these missions led to his being appointed chief pilot on "the pony express run" to supply B-29 bases in India by way of the Azores, Casablanca and Karachi. In time, he became commander of a ferry command squadron in India and personally flew supply missions across the Hump to bring the sinews of war to Chiang Kai-shek's embattled armies in China.

Supplies more exotic than war material were also delivered on occasion. Goldwater recalls that there was always great excitement and curiosity when word was received that a shipment was due for "Snow White." This was the code name of Madame Chiang Kai-shek, and the cargo that Goldwater and his pilots had to deliver ranged from personal accessories to refrigerators.

On one occasion, a fortune in Chinese currency printed in Philadelphia was shipped to Chiang. Goldwater, years later, recalled for Jack Bell, the Associated Press political correspondent in Washington, one flight in a C-54 loaded with several packing cases of currency and thirteen small kegs of gold. During the flight from Karachi to Imphal, India, Goldwater's crew began dreaming up fanciful ways in which they might dump the kegs and make off with the gold. Goldwater finally told them to knock if off because, though they had begun just by kidding about it, he recognized "crazy things can happen in wartime."

Goldwater brought this treasure-laden C-54 in for a landing at Imphal, not far from the war-torn Burma front, in a blinding rainstorm. The weather was so bad the ground crew refused to come out and unload the ship.

"I didn't like sitting on the ground there, the Japs were too close around for comfort," Goldwater later told Bell, "so I told the boys to open the hatches and dump the stuff out on the ramp. I'll never forget the sound as those thirteen kegs of gold clunked on the deck. We just left them there and got out as fast as we could."

When the war ended, Barry Goldwater had flown a lot of missions over the far reaches of vast oceans; he had delivered planes and war supplies to the fighting fronts; he had been so close to battle that he had seen the enemy, but he had never had a chance to shoot at them, nor they at him. He was a Lieutenant Colonel, and he flew a P-51 home to take up again the interrupted threads of his life.

Much evidence would seem to indicate that Barry Goldwater had relished his war experiences. Drawn to the military point of view ever since his boyhood training at Staunton, an activist always in love with danger, he had thrived on war's menu of challenge, excitement and far adventure; and he came out of it a fervid advocate of military power and a dedicated disciple of the Air Force, an organization he appears to feel can do no wrong.

For such a man, return to civilian life was a severe jolt. The management of Goldwater's was a tame and hum-drum business compared to the hazards of flying kegs of gold to Chiang Kai-shek. For Goldwater, life seemed to have lost much of its zest. He appeared "ill at ease and directionless" for some four years after the war, as Peggy Goldwater later told Alvin Toffler. He had "lost interest in the store," and he was obviously at loose ends, seeking some new activity to fill the void in his life, to renew the stimulation and challenge that war had provided.

The answer seemed to lie in civic activity. Goldwater

organized Arizona's Air National Guard, and he led the fight
to desegregate it. He interested himself in local causes in
Phoenix, and gradually, inevitably, he began to drift toward
the field of politics, a profession for which, it would seem,
his handsome appearance and personal magnetism had fitted
him.

Though Goldwater was late in taking the plunge into
politics, he had been fascinated from boyhood by the spectacle of political intrigue and political warfare. His indoctrination had come from his Uncle Morris, long the proprietor
of the Goldwater store in Prescott and a kingpin Democrat
in the state. As a boy, Goldwater would take himself off to
Prescott and sit in his uncle's store as soon as school was out,
listening to Morris spin tales of his political battles and of
the wily maneuverings in the state legislature.

Morris was a short, stocky, bald-headed man with a huge,
walrus-type mustache. Witty, a fascinating storyteller, a
joiner of virtually every civic and fraternal organization
under the Prescott sun, he had been enormously popular, and
he had served, off and on, for a total of twenty-three years
as Prescott's mayor. He had also seen service in the territorial legislature; he had been vice president of the state
constitutional convention and had played a prominent role
in drafting the state constitution when Arizona was admitted
to the Union. He had served several terms in the legislature,
having on occasion been a power in both its chambers as
Speaker of the House and President of the Senate.

One of Uncle Morris' fiercest political foes in the early days
had been William O. (Bucky) O'Neill, the Republican Sheriff
of Yapavai County. O'Neill and Morris Goldwater ran up
such a heated feud that, legend has it, they almost took
to their guns on one occasion to settle their differences.
When the Spanish-American War came along, however,
Bucky O'Neill went off to join Teddy Roosevelt's Rough
Riders and achieved a kind of immortality by being the
first man killed in the assault up San Juan Hill. His hero's
death wiped out memories of past unpleasantness, and back
in Prescott Morris Goldwater headed a committee that erected
an equestrian statue of Bucky O'Neill in the city square.
The story of the famous feud, of Bucky O'Neill's heroism
on San Juan Hill, had been heady fare for young Barry
Goldwater, who to this day lavishes a certain hero worship on
both O'Neill and his Uncle Morris.

In the days of Barry's youth, Uncle Morris was past his
office-holding prime, but he was still regarded as a political

patriarch and he attended all the major political rallies. His nephew would tag along with him, absorbing the atmosphere of politics along with much of Morris Goldwater's political ideology. These experiences had so profound an effect on Barry Goldwater that he has often said, "I was raised more by my uncle than by my father."

A favorite boast of Goldwater's is that his Uncle Morris "founded the Democratic Party in the Territory of Arizona," and there is much truth to it. Uncle Morris was certainly one of the party's principal architects. He considered himself a Jeffersonian Democrat; and, though Barry Goldwater concedes that "Jefferson was a liberal," he sees no conflict between his own arch-conservatism and his Uncle Morris' views. Uncle Morris, too, was a great believer in individual initiative, had great distrust of centralized governmental power, wanted no governmental interference in the affairs of business or the individual. "I grew up among conservative people, even though they were Democrats," Barry Goldwater has said. And he adds with absolute conviction: "If Uncle Morris knew what they were doing in the party today, he'd be doing snap rolls up in heaven."

One might have expected that, with such partisan Democratic heritage to guide him, Barry Goldwater would have joined the party of his Uncle Morris. One oft-repeated explanation of why he didn't goes this way: When Barry and Bob took over the family enterprises, they decided that it would be good business to play both sides of the street politically — for one to be a Republican and one to be a Democrat. So they flipped a coin to see who would be which, and the flip gave Barry to the Republicans. Goldwater insists now that this isn't so, that it never happened. He registered as a Republican, he says, because he felt like it, and Bob became a Democrat out of conviction.

In any event, the Goldwater brothers landed on opposite sides of the political fence; but in Arizona, where a rabid conservatism dominates much of the political landscape, party affiliations are often only a technicality. Bob and Barry think alike politically; and when Barry is running for office, the whole Goldwater clan is united in his support.

Goldwater first wet his toes in the political waters the year after the war ended. In 1946, he began heading various civic projects spurring the growth of a greater Phoenix. This growth quickly became associated with an anti-union issue — the passage of a state right-to-work law.

Unions had never been strong in Arizona, a largely nonindustrial state, but they had been trying to organize and to get a stronger toehold. Phoenix businessmen, feeling the first surges of the boom they were to ride to true metropolitan status, were anxious to attract new industries. They felt certain that a strong lure would be the passage of a law banning the closed shop, the bulwark of powerful unionism. Organizers of the drive approached Goldwater and asked if he would head the retailers' division in the campaign to pressure passage of so-called right-to-work legislation. Goldwater agreed and jumped into the heart of the fray.

A businessman, head of a department store empire, Goldwater had long been concerned about the growing power of unions. He has always endeavored to put this attitude on the plane of principle, divorced from the selfish considerations of his own business class. He is opposed, he says, to any man's being compelled to join a union in order to get work; he argues that a man should have an opportunity to hunt and get any available job, and if he wants to join a union of his own free will, that's all right. The fact that, under such a system, unions inevitably confer their benefits on a lot of free riders, faint hearts on whom they cannot count in any showdown, makes no impression on Goldwater. He argues that the closed shop leads to union boss dictatorship and that unions will be more cleanly and efficiently operated if they have to win converts rather than compel them. So believing, he sat down in 1946 and drafted a strongly worded letter that he sent to retail executives, urging that they get behind the right-to-work campaign. Union leaders obtained a copy of the letter and promptly denounced Goldwater as anti-labor, a charge that has dogged him ever since. But right-to-work, backed in conservative Arizona by the powerful business community, received the approval of the legislature and became the law of the state.

Goldwater's next thrust into politics came in 1949. In that year, a group of fifty Phoenix citizens organized an independent movement to oust the entrenched machine that had been running affairs from City Hall for years. There was no major political scandal, no disclosures of graft on which the "outs" might feed, but there were what they considered examples of bumbling and ineptitude. They decided to draft a slate for City Council and to campaign on the promise of running the city's affairs with businesslike efficiency. A leader in the movement was Goldwater's boyhood friend Harry Rosenzweig, and when it came time to name candidates to oppose the machine, Goldwater's name was high on every man's list.

He had headed highly successful Red Cross and Community Chest drives, and had been named Phoenix' Man of the Year for 1949. It seemed he was a natural.

At first, Goldwater turned down the proposition cold. It would be bad for the store, he said, for him to get so directly involved in politics; he was too busy — and he was no politician. Afterward, thinking it over, Goldwater began to reconsider. He felt that he, like a lot of other businessmen, had done a tremendous amount of griping about governmental inefficiency; how, he says he asked himself, were things ever going to change if men like himself refused to stand for office? So when Rosenzweig returned to the attack and urged him to fill out the ticket, Goldwater changed his mind and accepted.

He explained his decision in a letter he wrote the next day to his brother, Bob, and to Bill Saufley, the other member of the store's ruling triumvirate. He wrote:

"Willie and Bob:

"You both will probably think me seven kinds of a dirty bastard when you hear that I have decided to run for councilman along with Harry and the rest and I dont [sic] blame you much. The heat was put on me quite heavily and with no support during both your abscences [sic] I gave in. However I dont [sic] think a man can live with himself when he asks others to do his dirty work for him. I couldn't criticize the government of this city when I myself refused to help. I dont [sic] know if we can win but if we do then I know Phoenix will have two years of damned good government that I hope will set a pattern for the coming years and the coming generations. There has always been one and sometimes two Goldwaters damned fools enough to get into politics and they always did it with service in their minds which is the way I approach this thing . . . .

"Dont [sic] cuss me too much. It ain't for life and it may be fun."

Once he had made his decision, Goldwater went all-out to win. He campaigned from door to door, shook hands, made countless speeches. He proved from the outset, of course, that he had been made to order for the political wars; the charm that had caused a near riot among the female populace of Phoenix when the young Barry manned the piece-goods counter in Goldwater's was just as devastating when it was turned on the voters. The reformers won, and Goldwater led the ticket, with his friend, Harry Rosenzweig, not far behind.

Goldwater's two terms on the Phoenix City Council (he was re-elected in 1951) were marked by some uncompromising stands. One of his first major projects was the desegregation of eating facilities at the municipally owned Phoenix Sky Harbor Airport. Though Goldwater in 1964 was to vote against the civil rights bill, a stand that put him on the side of the Southern segregationists and white supremacists, he, personally, has never displayed any racial prejudice. As a boy he had played and boxed with John Henry Lewis, and he has often said that he never heard of racial prejudice until he went to Staunton. Much evidence seems to indicate that he could not have liked what he saw and heard then. For just as he had been instrumental in forcing the desegregation of the Arizona Air National Guard, so now he accomplished the desegregation of Phoenix' airport facilities.

The apparent paradox between his personal and his public attitudes reflects, like much else about Goldwater, his uncompromising and ultra-simple faith in individual initiative as the cure-all of every problem — and his accompanying detestation of governmental initiative in almost any form. Illustrative of this fetish was his attitude regarding the parking problem in Phoenix. Like virtually every other major city, Phoenix was plagued by utterly inadequate parking facilities in its downtown business district. And so the proposal was made that the city should undertake to provide parking. Goldwater, who as a downtown merchant would have benefited from the project, would have none of it. The way to handle the problem, he opined, was for the downtown merchants to get together and build their own parking facility. Many of the merchants, needless to say, did not agree with Goldwater that rugged individualism must, of necessity, be all *that* rugged.

These experiences on the Phoenix City Council merely whetted Goldwater's long dormant appetite for politics. He began to look to broader horizons. His view was influenced by his reading and study of his family's early struggles and the history of Arizona. Big Mike and Little Joe and Uncle Morris had been true pioneers in the settlement and development of wild territory, and at one time or another Goldwaters, Uncle Morris especially, had held virtually every office within the gift of the electorate except governor. Barry Goldwater thought this was an omission that should be rectified.

He had struck up a friendship with Howard Pyle, a radio commentator with a great following in Phoenix. Arizona traditionally had been overwhelmingly Democratic, but Pyle, sensing a change, confided to Goldwater that he thought 1950 would be a good year for Republicanism. The two laid their plans accordingly. They agreed that Goldwater would run for governor in 1950 and that Pyle would seek the U. S. Senate post two years later.

A chance event disrupted this schedule. Pyle was invited to address a statewide meeting of Young Republicans, and he was so eloquent he stampeded the youthful herd. When he finished speaking, they clamored for him to become the party's candidate for governor. Though this development shelved his own ambitions, Goldwater took it good naturedly and threw himself into the battle as Pyle's campaign manager.

Goldwater is nothing if not a battler; he goes all-out to meet every challenge as if the fate of the world depended on the outcome. In his lexicon, second place doesn't count. It doesn't even rate a tombstone. All that matters is to win. This attitude was probably never more vividly displayed than in the 1950 campaign. Goldwater punished himself and Pyle unmercifully. He forced the campaign in the hot Arizona summer and kept at it day after day right through the fall. He and Pyle put bedrolls in Goldwater's Beech Bonanza, and they practically lived in the plane. With Goldwater at the controls, they logged more than 50,000 miles, flitting into virtually every hamlet, shaking innumerable hands, making countless speeches. And in November, when the votes were tallied, they had their reward; Pyle squeaked in. The narrowness of his victory did not matter; what mattered was that he had won and, in winning, had broken the Democratic stranglehold on Arizona politics.

Pyle's victory paved the way for Barry Goldwater to make his move in 1952. Yet, even though he had Pyle's triumph to build on, Goldwater's task seemed, at first glance, all but impossible. When he entered the race for the U. S. Senate, he had for his opponent Ernest W. McFarland, a veteran Arizona Democrat and champion vote-getter. McFarland also carried into the campaign enormous prestige deriving from the fact that he had become the Senate Majority Leader, a post of no small power and influence, one that Arizona voters might be expected to want to retain for their own. Given the normally heavy Democratic majorities in the state, hardly anyone in Arizona gave Barry Goldwater even a fighting chance.

Such handicapping, though it had a superficial logic about it, ignored substratum realities about two parties to this affair — Arizona and Barry Goldwater.

CHAPTER VII

Phoenix Country Club McCarthy

The phenomenon of Barry Goldwater can be understood only if one understands Arizona itself. It is a state with the brand of the frontier still upon it; a state whose wide-open spaces and relatively sparse population have cultivated the feeling that the individual is king; a state lacking in the problems of the mass society that afflict so much of the rest of the nation. In Arizona the race problem is not a crucial issue, for there are relatively few Negroes. Mass transit and urban renewal are words without meaning, for there are no sprawling, interstate metropolitan complexes and few cities so old and slum-infested as to need major rehabilitation. Landlocked, isolated, a rural state still in the process of growth and development from the raw frontier, Arizona is essentially self-centered, more vitally concerned with issues of her own expansion than with such remote problems as trade with Communist nations, or the functioning of the U. N., or the existence of vast depressed areas that President Johnson would eliminate by his war on poverty.

As is the state, so are the people. The older stock, like the Goldwaters, are descended from first settlers who struck it rich and stayed. Some of these are cattle barons, still suspicious like their forebears of "Eastern dudes." Others are the heirs of the early mining and railroad empire builders. To these have been added new and powerful executive classes — rulers of the electronics industry that has accounted for much of the mushrooming growth, and construction tycoons who have waxed rich in the process of quadrupling the size of Phoenix since 1950. These dominant segments of Arizona society are reinforced by others. Arizona's hot, dry and healthful climate attracts the ill, the retired rich and middle-class.

The scions of the old families, the new executive classes making their fortunes fast in the boom, the owners of new industries seeking an oasis against strong unionism, the rich retired and the moderately well-off retired, all are united in the blood brotherhood of selfish and potent fixations. They hate spending for foreign aid, for this is remote from their interests, which are strictly parochial. They hate the progressive income tax, for this drains their fast-accumulating or accumulated wealth. They hate big government and big spending programs, for these mean higher taxes and may cause inflation. They want nothing so much as for government to leave them alone in their haven, in their own special wonderland of mountains, deserts and jagged canyons.

This is a society that, not unnaturally, expresses itself in the fanatical voice of the Radical Right — and, in its innocence, considers the raucous tones of fanaticism the essence of sweet reason. The John Birch Society and the Minutemen flourish in this fertile soil. And the bias they spread is everywhere. Consider the furor that erupted when it was announced that Max Lerner, college professor and columnist for *The New York Post*, was to appear on television in Phoenix. Though Lerner is anything but a radical, the announcement that he was about to invade Phoenix was like waving a red flag before the distended eyes of the conservative bulls. Irate citizens wrote letters of protest, denouncing him as a dangerous radical because he held "internationalist" views.

The spirit of Phoenix is capsuled in such incidents. A woman who is herself a leader of Phoenix society confesses that she had to wage a hard battle with her conscience before she could bring herself to support the United Nations. In her family and in the social circles in which she moved, she said, she heard nothing but condemnation of the world organization. Fanaticism, she pointed out, extends even into the realm of health, for the Birchers and Minutemen had denounced the local health organization as "a communist plot."

"The thinking goes this way," this woman explained. "The Birchers claim that if mental health groups get powerful and if they are dominated by left-wingers and communists, they will railroad all the Birchers into the mental hospitals."

But perhaps the epitome of radical rightism in Phoenix was reached in the feverish flowering of the anti-anti-anti-Communist agitation. The reasoning here becomes a bit tortuous for the uninitiated, and it may be necessary to go slow to get it. But it runs like this: anti-Communists, of course, are on the side of God and the angels — they are very, very good. It follows, then, that anyone who opposes them — in other words, an "anti-anti" — is taking the part of the devil — he (though he may only be an innocent soul objecting to frenzy) is very, very bad. Since no sane man wants to place himself in the devil's corner, such loudly proclaimed reasoning crimps the style of all but the most courageous dissidents; it leaves, indeed, precious little room for reason or debate. But that, in Phoenix, is considered just the way it should be.

Such was the milieu that produced Barry Goldwater. And Barry, who himself acknowledges that he has never been a deep thinker, fits into this society as the hand fits into the glove.

"Barry follows in the family tradition," one Phoenix doctor who knows him well told Herbert Black of *The Boston Globe*. "In his philosophy the world is still open for those who have the courage to open it. His family suffered setbacks and defeats. He thinks this is the path for America to follow to remain strong.

"The only thing wrong with this independence is that without the Federal dams in the mountains there wouldn't be any water here, and Phoenix and Goldwater's store would both be small."

It is one of the ironies of life in the great Southwest that this elementary truth goes so absolutely unappreciated, indeed unrecognized. Probably no section of the country owes more to federal spending. Arizona has battened on it for years. Literally *billions* of dollars have been lavished on federal dams in a program stretching back to the progressive regime of Theodore Roosevelt, and these immense projects have brought water to what was parched and arid desert, turning wastes into blooming farmlands. Goldwater, of course, has always advocated such types of "reclamation" projects for his beloved Arizona. Just the use of that simple word "reclamation" seems to sanctify such endeavors and set them apart in his mind as somehow different from other forms of federal spending. A different kind of "reclamation" project for the poverty-ridden Appalachian area brings from him a roar of outrage about the dangers of rampant socialism, and it seems never to have occurred to him — and he appears genuinely astonished that it should occur to others — that there is any collision of principle between this stand and his advocacy of federal aid instead of sturdy "do-it-yourself" for Arizona.

Only a man of basically simple mind, satisfied with his own prejudices and unaware of intellectual issues, could miss the point so completely and innocently. This in itself tells much about Goldwater. He is a man who has imbibed beliefs from his associates and surroundings instead of arriving at them by the process of examination and intellectual struggle. *The New York Times* in a profile, January 4, 1964, put it this way:

"His convictions don't come from deep thinking or from the friction and hard knocks of experience. He never thought seriously about politics until he was elected to the Senate in the Eisenhower landslide of 1952. He brought along with him dogmas and prejudices he picked up as a prosperous businessman in Phoenix, from its Rotary and Country Club and boards of directors' meetings.

" 'I just think he has never bothered to test his ideas very strenuously. He's comfortable with them, and of course he has found that a lot of other people find them attractive, too. It looks like a good combination, so he has stuck with it,' one associate has said."

In the Arizona of today, the trends of 1952, when Barry Goldwater first sought election to the Senate against Ernest McFarland, have been deepened. The state has grown much faster; its prejudices have intensified; its peculiar, blind brand of conservatism has hardened and become more obvious through the overt activities of the Birchers and the Minutemen. What was latent has become blatant.

Barry Goldwater himself, despite his charm and his air of sweet reasonableness, has been from the first fully in tune with this development. Even before he had held a major political office or had a chance to take a stand on national issues, he was recognized and embraced by some of the strongest ultra-right forces in America. Their affection was expressed in the way that counted most, through some lusty financial contributions to Goldwater's first campaign. The genesis of this love affair has never been spelled out. The Goldwaters, of course, frequently vacationed at their summer home in La Jolla, California, long a watering place and favorite stamping ground for financiers of the ultra right. The Murchisons of Texas ran a large motel there; Sid Richardson and other Texas tycoons made it a favorite rendezvous; and there are indications that Goldwater circulated in this social strata and that his views on free enterprise and government interference were known and appreciated by its members.

The fact is emphasized when one examines a list of the financial contributors to Goldwater's campaigns. The Murchisons and Sid Richardson have helped. So has Joseph Pew, Sun Oil tycoon and underwriter of right-wing causes. In the 1952 campaign, Goldwater later reported contributions of $44,721 to McFarland's $24,455. Significantly, more than half this Goldwater money came from wealthy backers outside his own state of Arizona. H. L. Hunt, the Texas oil billionaire who is sometimes called the richest man in the world, sent $3,000. Other well-heeled Texans posted an additional $8,000. The ultra-conservative Americans for America, of Chicago, tossed another $3,000 into the pot. It would certainly seem that, even this early, the angels of the far right had established an affinity with the man who in the next dozen years was to become their spokesman.

The kind of campaign that Goldwater ran against McFarland speaks volumes. It was the campaign of a Phoenix Country Club McCarthy.

Goldwater pictured himself as the champion of the "American Idea" in mortal battle with the "Socialist Idea" — a label he pinned on McFarland. This bit of demagogy enabled Goldwater to wrap himself in the folds of the flag and to invoke the assistance of God and all the heavenly angels in his crusade against the dark and mysterious forces of evil.

McFarland, of course, was no more a socialist than Willam McKinley had been. A ruddy, kind-faced man, he was an amiable, unaggressive, moderate, conservative, and he had risen to his post as Senate Majority Leader not by any special drive of his own, but simply through the process of attrition and succession. To drape the socialist tag about the neck of such a plodding old political warhorse might have been ludicrous if it had not been so insidiously and damnably effective.

In more than a thousand speeches, delivered in every section of the state and from every available rostrum, Goldwater pumped away at his favorite theme with a passion and an evident sincerity that impressed his audiences. He painted the "Democrat Party" (he never called it the Democratic Party, a form of derogation that was supposed to have some significance) as being a war party and yet, at the same time, somehow, "soft on communism." He excoriated "Trumanism" for "coddling Communists in government." Joe McCarthy himself might have done the deed with shriller ranting, but he couldn't have spread the tar much more effectively.

Having painted McFarland into this red-dyed corner, Goldwater thundered on against all the things he and all Arizona's arch-conservatives hated. He was against a huge federal monstrosity invading the domain of the states. He was against foreign aid and federal proposals for aid to education. He was against the growing power of labor, against huge welfare expenditures, against federal public works projects. He was, in a word, against the whole pattern of federal government as it had developed in the twentieth century.

As Emmet John Hughes, the gifted speech writer for Eisenhower, was later to point out in his *The Ordeal of Power*, the Republicans in this campaign developed an infinite and dangerous capacity for believing even the most outrageous excesses of their own propaganda. Goldwater was no exception. He had a passionate faith in the validity of his own prejudices. "Probably neither Goldwater nor McFarland could have defined the socialist idea at the time," Jack Bell wrote later, but this didn't matter. Goldwater through the years has demonstrated a virtually complete incapacity to distinguish between liberalism on the one hand and socialism and communism on the other. All liberals are to him "radicals," and though they may not be conscious traitors (he is generously willing to admit they may not be aware of the evil they do), they are no less dangerous for that.

The technique, first tried out in this 1952 campaign against McFarland, produced devastating results. McFarland simply did not have the personal dynamism to counter the barrage to which he was subjected. He was a baby-kisser and hand-shaker. His speeches were pedestrian, dull and uninspired. And when he was subjected to the exposure of television, the effect was almost embarrassing. Television made McFarland seem an ineffectual bumbler; and, by contrast, it magnified Barry Goldwater's handsomeness and projected that vibrant glamor-boy quality of his. To all this, there was added a further and decidedly unfair handicap. Handsome Barry Goldwater was riding the coattails of war-hero Eisenhower, and McFarland had to try to shoulder the assorted debris and frustrations of the Truman administration.

Poor McFarland. At the outset of the campaign, the odds on his winning had been quoted at 5 to 1, with few takers, but as election day neared, it became apparent there was a ground swell running in favor of the underdog. When the votes were counted, it was found that Eisenhower had carried the state by 43,000 — and Goldwater had defeated McFarland by 7,000 votes.

Goldwater, with that candor about himself that is one of his most attractive traits, frankly acknowledged: "I rode Ike's coattails."

But, before many years had passed, he was to be attacking the man whose coattails he had ridden.

CHAPTER VIII

Taft and Goldwater

When Barry Goldwater went to Washington as a freshman Senator in 1953, he had one great political hero, Senator Robert A. Taft, of Ohio, "Mr. Republican" to a whole generation of his party. It was to Taft far more than to Eisenhower, that Goldwater felt he owed his political allegiance. In one of those paradoxes in which history and politics delight, Taft and Goldwater were superficially alike in some of their cardinal tenets, but greatly unlike in ability and method, in vision and in the comprehension of national issues. Their first meeting, though neither of them could have realized it at the time, symbolized a divergence of conservative patterns. Taft, the responsible conservative who was so soon to die of cancer, was about to pass on the mantle of doctrinaire leadership to the young Senator from Arizona, a man who was not a true conservative by many of Taft's own standards, but a country club radical rightist.

The essential difference between the two men may be put most simply. Taft had a quick, alert, intelligent mind, with a comprehensive grasp of all facets of public issues as he saw them; temperamentally, he disliked many of the trends of the twentieth century, but realistically and intellectually he recognized that the century existed and that many of its developments were inevitable. Goldwater, on the other hand, has a very limited intellectual range and an imperfect grasp of detail. In a party caucus, Taft was a driving force, coherent, cogent, familiar with the minutiae of every crucial issue and decision; Goldwater, by contrast, most often sits and listens, contributing little, a glaze of boredom soon casting its dull film over his eyes. Unlike Taft's, Goldwater's reaction and understanding of public issues is visceral.

Taft could and did at times sound almost like Goldwater. Take, for example, a Chicago speech in 1953 in which he decried the over-emphasis on the free enterprise system because this gave the false impression that all its advocates were concerned about was business freedom. This, Taft asserted, simply was not so. The real issue was liberty. Taft said:

"Liberty means the liberty of every individual to live his own life and to think his own thoughts, to have those thoughts taught by someone, if anyone can be found who thinks they are worth teaching; the liberty of our families to spend the money which they earn on the things that they want for their family instead of turning it over to the government to be used in providing government services they may or may not want, and probably won't get.

"I don't believe you can have freedom in a country the size of the United States unless you have freedom of state and local communities to decide their own affairs. This country is so tremendous that no one sitting in Washington is responsive to local public opinion and consequently the regulations he attempts to make amount to tyranny in many communities where they are different from what the people want."

Such a creed, with its emphasis on individual freedom, its deprecation of big federal government, its appeal for states' rights and local initiative, is a pure revelation of the true faith as Goldwater sees it.

But Taft, in action, sometimes clouded the ideal with what Goldwater considered the corruption of "me-tooism." Taft was practical enough and intelligent enough to recognize that the mass, industrialized society of the twentieth century is far different from the simpler, agrarian world of the nineteenth; and he understood that, in such a complex existence, there were things that the government *had* to do for the people because the people could not do them for themselves. Taft would fight to slow down the trend toward ever larger government, but he appreciated that the trend itself was inevitable. Such understanding of the realities of his world, however, would lead Taft, as it had back in the 1940's, to sponsor federal housing programs and aid to education, projects that in the 1960's are still anathema to Goldwater.

The pillars of Goldwater's Radical Right support doubtless would shatter and fall should the Arizona Senator ever give expression to the kind of sentiments Taft revealed in a 1948 speech in which he said:

"In matters affecting the necessities of life — and I should like to confine it to the necessities of life; namely, to relief, to education, to health and to housing — I do not believe the federal government can say it has no interest, and say to the people, 'Go your way and do the best you can.'

"I do not believe that. Because the way wealth is distributed in the United States I think we have a responsibility to see if we cannot eliminate hardship, poverty and inequality to the best of our ability. I do not believe we are able to do it without a federal aid system."

Regarding federal aid to education, Taft was especially emphatic. There was, he said, "nothing more important," and he added that "I know of no way of going forward in that field to any substantial degree without providing some federal assistance."

Goldwater, on the other hand, could tell a Jacksonville, Fla., political rally during the 1960 fall campaign:

"The government has no right to educate children. The parents, you and I, have that responsibility. The child has no right to an education. In most cases the children will get along very well without it."

Goldwater contended afterward, as he so often does, that he had been incorrectly quoted in the press. What he had meant to say, he explained, was that a child does not have "a right" to an education; he has only "the liberty" to go and seek it. This fine distinction hardly beclouds the essential fact — that Goldwater, unlike Taft, opposes federal aid to education in any form.

Such were the differences between the two men, each of whom was to stand in his time as representative of the Republican Party.

Taft, in their brief association, set Goldwater's feet on the path he was to follow and pointed him at a principal target — labor unions. Goldwater, ever the military enthusiast, had hoped for appointment to the Senate Armed Services Committee. He argued that his war experience and his continued activity as a reserve officer (he is now a Major General in the Air Force Reserve) had given him a certain expertise in military affairs that would be useful. Taft, however, assigned Goldwater to the Labor Committee. Republicans, he said, wanted a good solid businessman on that committee, and they were convinced Goldwater was the man. This was perhaps an indication that Goldwater's advocacy of right-to-work in 1946 had been remembered upstairs, where memory counts, and it was perhaps a further indication that Goldwater's powerful backers in the 1952 campaign were making certain that their boy was being placed where he could do them the most good.

Though one may never fully know the murky ways by which influence makes itself felt in politics, it is abundantly clear that there were powerful hidden forces that, from the start, considered Barry Goldwater on the side of the angels. A freshman Senator coming from a sparsely populated Southwestern state, with only a handful of electoral votes and virtually no influence, could hardly expect in the normal course of events to become an instantaneous power in Washington. Normally, it would take years of hard work and careful building of his image before he would even be recognized. It seems significant that things did not work out this way at all with Barry Goldwater.

Jack Bell, in his biography of Goldwater, relates the previously untold story of the secret machinations that shelved amendments to the Taft-Hartley Act. This measure, much hated by labor, had been an issue in the 1952 campaign. Both parties had pledged alterations in some of the Act's more restrictive provisions, and Eisenhower had wooed labor support with this promise. In an apparent attempt to implement this pledge, he had named Martin P. Durkin, former president of the A.F.L. plumber's union, as his first Secretary of Labor. Durkin, a decided misfit in a cabinet composed largely of millionaires, prepared a series of nineteen proposed changes in the Taft-Hartley Act and won Eisenhower's endorsement of his program.

It was at this point, according to Bell, that freshman Senator Barry Goldwater, newly named to the Labor Committee by Taft, received an emergency telephone call to come to a conference with Vice President Richard M. Nixon. He found Nixon studying a message from Eisenhower that he had been directed to present to the Senate the next day. The message spelled out Durkin's proposed Taft-Hartley amendments and called for action on them. Nixon showed Goldwater the Presidential draft and asked for his opinion. Goldwater promptly gave it. He didn't like the proposals at all.

Nixon said he didn't either. In fact, he disliked the whole business so strongly he was going to disobey Eisenhower's instructions and hold up the whole message. This brash tactic was the beginning of a delaying action that was to be completely successful. Republican powers went to work on Eisenhower in secret. Durkin protested personally to Eisenhower, and Eisenhower, he said afterward, assured him he was all for the Durkin program; Durkin could rest assured it would be presented to Congress. But it never was. Durkin's plan had popped, not into the Congressional hopper under the aegis of the President of the United States, but into the secretly fashioned Nixon-Goldwater pigeonhole. Congress adjourned without ever getting the message it was supposed to have received. Feeling betrayed, Durkin resigned, freeing the cabinet of millionaires of his disturbing presence.

The incident tells much about Barry Goldwater. Newly arrived in Washington, never before active in politics above the level of the Phoenix City Council, he had been called to consultation with the Vice President of the United States; his advice had been sought and evidently considered important — with the result that a Presidential message had been filed and forgotten and that a Secretary of Labor in the President's cabinet had been forced to resign. It seems safe to say that not many freshmen Senators, only a few months in Washington, get admitted to the inner councils so quickly.

Where labor was concerned, however, Barry Goldwater was like a nuclear-tipped rocket. All anybody had to do was to aim him and push the button — and he would go off. Goldwater partisans, of course, will take violent exception to this statement. In recent years, with the image of the Presidency dancing before his eyes, Goldwater has made earnest efforts to fudge the record and pose as the great friend of the laboring man. He argues that all he has ever wanted to do is to protect honest unionists from boss dictation; all he has ever wanted is to reform the unions, not cripple the labor movement. Goldwater, with his salesman's personality, always sounds plausible and convincing; but when one stops listening to his words and studies his acts, the record doesn't read the way he contends it reads.

Take, for example, one of the most intemperate — and significant — of his early performances in this field. This occurred in the fall of 1955, and again the year is important. For in this year, still a newcomer to Washington, with less than two years' service in the Senate to his credit, Goldwater had been named chairman of the Republican Senatorial Campaign Committee, a key party post carrying with it enormous prestige and influence. The man who holds this job is thrown automatically into contact with county and state chairmen throughout the nation; the ties of party organization are in his hands; and he has an admirable springboard for future ambitions. Barry Goldwater, in 1955, had been bequeathed the springboard, and he used it with characteristic, partisan energy to launch a blistering, attention-attracting attack on labor and the Democrats.

He prepared a report which was circulated among GOP party workers. It pictured labor as engaging in a horrendous conspiracy which was about to subvert the Constitution and take over the nation.

Goldwater accused union leaders of planning for the "massive use of political slush funds — on a nationwide scale" to insure the outcome of the 1956 election. They were participating in a "conspiracy of national proportions." There had been "increasingly ruthless and successful efforts of certain elements in the leadership of labor unions to take over and control the Democratic Party." In Michigan "CIO goon squads" armed with guns and clubs had wrested control of the party from the rank-and-file in 1950 in a conspiracy that was "by no means unique."

"The use of violence and coercion by union leaders . . . has now been transferred from the area of industrial disputes and brought boldly into purely political areas," Goldwater proclaimed.

The Baltimore *Sun,* commenting on this performance, noted that Republicans appeared to be attempting the incredible feat of trying to woo labor votes on the one hand while they blackened labor leadership on the other. For this seeming paradox, Goldwater had a facile explanation. He argued that some 40 percent of union members were devout Republicans who were being compelled, in order to hold their jobs, to contribute campaign funds to the Democrats. The newly formed AFL-CIO, he shouted, should have "no right" to endorse a Presidential candidate in 1956 because such action would "infringe" on the rights of that stalwart 40 percent in their ranks who were Republicans.

This was the diatribe. In the perspective of history, it looks pretty silly because Goldwater's labor "goon squad" bogeymen never have materialized and have yet to take over the Democratic Party. Even at the time, though Goldwater's anti-union fantasy made some headlines about the country in a press that is receptive to such charges, the specifics were so flimsy that the whole tissue began to fall apart at the first breath of examination.

On what did Goldwater base his assertion that 40 percent of union members were Republican? On what did he base his charge that labor "goon squads" armed with guns and clubs were going to take over the Democratic Party? What was the evidence about labor's raising of a "massive" slush fund for 1956?

Goldwater in his tract to Republican workers had attempted to give his charges authenticity by citing "a recent survey made by the Union Education Service, Chicago University, in association with Cornell and Columbia researchers." This survey, he said, actually showed that "41 percent of union labor questioned is Republican."

John McCollum, director of the University of Chicago's Research and Education Projects (and so the man in charge of the supposed survey), promptly revealed that there were no statistics to justify Goldwater's assertion that 40 percent of union members were Republicans. "We have never asked that kind of question . . . in any of our surveys," he said. ". . . We have asked union members if they would like to see their unions lined up with a political party and seldom has the response for the Republicans been more than four or five percent — the average, I would say, is around one or two per cent."

Goldwater had also said the survey showed 43 percent of union members felt their unions should take no part in politics. McCollum explained there was just no basis for such an assertion. He acknowledged his researchers had polled 338 members of the Oil Workers Union in Lemont, Ill., and 43 per cent of this small local union had said they did not want their local to take an "active part" in politics. Other locals polled in the state survey, however, McCollum added, had voted overwhelmingly in favor of union political activity. It seemed quite clear that Goldwater, ignoring the broader and more significant facts, had based a sweeping national generalization upon some figures gleaned in a study of just 338 members belonging to one small local in one small Illinois town.

Goldwater's horror picture of "violence and coercion" and an army of labor goons usurping power in the Democratic Party didn't fare any better when exposed to the daylight. These sweeping charges were based, as Goldwater's office acknowledged, on a book, *The CIO and the Democratic Party*, written by Fay Calkins, described by Goldwater as "an analyst" for labor's Political Action Committee itself. Miss Calkins' book dealt with the 1950 takeover of the Democratic Party in Michigan by a "liberal coalition" in which labor had played a conspicuous part. According to Miss Calkins, a "small clique of Old Guard Democrats with a patronage outlook" had been in control of the party and had been running it steadily downhill prior to the liberal-labor coalition's attack. The coalition was described as a "grass roots" movement that had resulted in the filing of petitions to contest the election of precinct captains in Detroit. Examination of the Old Guard's counter-petitions by the insurgents showed that they were decorated with many a name taken straight from the tombstones. The liberal faction challenged these signatures from the world beyond the grave and demanded the Old Guard justify them or get out. The Old Guard got. There was in Miss Calkins' book just one incident that seemed to bear any relation to Goldwater's sensational charges about "goon squads" and "violence and coercion." One precinct worker had told Miss Calkins that he had gone to a meeting equipped for trouble, lugging two pistols and a club — but no trouble had developed, and no guns or clubs had been used. Goldwater evidently had magnified preparation into event and had used the event that never happened to create the specter of the impending takeover of the entire Democratic Party by an army of labor thugs.

This left only the slush fund. There wasn't much doubt that a large segment of labor, especially after the Martin Durkin double cross by the Eisenhower administration on its Taft-Hartley pledges, would back the Democrats in 1956. But Goldwater had been ranting about a "massive" slush fund that, at a minimum, would amount to some $1.8 million and might go as high as $10 million. What evidence was there of this?

James L. McDevitt, regional director of Labor's League for Political Education, accused Goldwater of either ignorance or deliberate falsehood. He pointed out that the League, from the time it was formed in 1948 through Sept. 2, 1955, had spent exactly $1,788,669.23, a far cry from raising millions in one year for one campaign. On the other hand, McDevitt pointed out, Senator Taft, by his own official accounting, had spent $1,905,509.61 in his 1950 re-election campaign in the state of Ohio alone. Other unreported Taft expenditures were rumored to have swelled the Senator's overall "slush fund" to about $5 million, McDevitt said, and he wondered out loud why Senator Goldwater wasn't exercised about this. As for the Labor League, McDevitt said, it had received just $132,585.22 in the past year in voluntary contributions from union workers. Was this, he asked, a "massive" slush fund? "How little is 'massive?'" he taunted, in ridicule of Goldwater.

Such devastating exposure might have been expected to disturb a man as scrupulous as Goldwater is supposed to be. But there is no sign that it ever fazed Goldwater in the slightest. He was to go on and on over the years, thundering his denunciations of the labor "menace" and stepping up the tempo of his charges against his own personal bête noire, Walter Reuther, the powerful president of CIO's United Automobile Workers. It was a pattern of conduct that says much. Barry Goldwater, handsome, personable, engaging as he is on the personal level, is a ruthless politician on the stump. Goldwater always runs for first place. To win is the thing, and the means to be used are not always scrupulously selected.

Perhaps nothing demonstrated this more clearly than Goldwater's fervent admiration of Joe McCarthy and his unhesitating adoption of the McCarthy technique of smear and innuendo in running down a political opponent.

CHAPTER IX

In the Footsteps of McCarthy

In the winter of 1950, a few weeks after the conviction of Alger Hiss for perjury, a relatively unknown Senator from Wisconsin rose to his feet in the boondocks of West Virginia, and waving aloft a piece of paper, he proclaimed with the snarl that was to send shivers up and down the spine of America, "I have here in my hand" evidence that literally hundreds of employees in the State Department were Communists. Joseph R. McCarthy was later to confide to friends, chuckling hugely at his own cleverness and audacity, that he had had in his hand at the moment no document more evidentiary than a used laundry slip. It did not matter. The reckless and irresponsible charge, echoed by a partisan press, resounded across the land as if written in holy script, and soon Americans were listening to the daily, accusatory bellows of the junior Senator from Wisconsin, convinced that traitors in high places were selling out the national birthright.

So powerful a rabble-rouser did Joe McCarthy become that the Republicans in 1952, having no scruples where votes were concerned, rushed to embrace both him and his techniques. The wilder his charges against the Democratic regime of Harry Truman, the greater became his asset to the Grand Old Party, and literally nothing that he said or did could stir the soul of Republicanism to repugnance.

Joe McCarthy, it seemed, could do no wrong. He bestrode the American scene, a colossus of innuendo, a human whirlwind of suspicion and smear, generating his own force by his ever more reckless charges, superior to and contemptuous of every agency of government. Inevitably, he finally went too far, even for this time and this crusade. He launched a brutal attack upon the Army, claiming it, too, was riddled by subversive influences, and he compounded all of his offenses by lashing out at a fellow Republican, Senator

70

Robert C. Hendrickson of New Jersey, as "a living miracle without brains or guts." When he turned on his fellow Senators, he committed the unforgivable offense. The Senate moved to censure.

Barry Goldwater took his stand for Joe McCarthy. He had known McCarthy for fourteen years and liked him. Joe was a friend, and in Goldwater's view, all Joe had done was to fight communism. And what was wrong with that?

Before Goldwater rose in the Senate to take part in the McCarthy censure debate in November, 1954, the battle lines had been clearly drawn. McCarthy, ever the demagogue, had wrapped himself in the folds of the flag and attacked his attackers. He had charged that the only reason the censure motion had been brought was that "for some years I have been exposing communists." He thundered that the censure committee headed by Senator Arthur V. Watkins, Utah Republican, had become the "unwilling handmaiden" of the Communist Party. He did not go so far as to say that the committee "knowingly did the work" of communism, but it had become "the victim of a Communist campaign; and having been victimized, it became the party's involuntary agent."

Senator John C. Stennis, the Mississippi Democrat held in high esteem by his peers in the Senate, had stressed the opposing view.

"Is it a sufficient answer to say 'Joe McCarthy has done some good in hunting communists?'" he asked. "Shall we destroy what have been considered the necessary processes in carrying out one mission because a man has done good in another field, on another mission? I cannot assent to such an argument."

This mild appeal to reason did not move Goldwater. All that mattered to him was the preservation of the anti-communist witch-hunt, the emotional ingredient that fueled the flames of the ultra-conservative movement. Goldwater made the point abundantly clear when he said he could not recall, in any of the speeches that had been made, "any serious facing of the key issue which we are called upon to settle in this session — the question of what will happen to America's fight against communism if the efforts of a man who has been active in the fight against this evil are repudiated."

Goldwater went further. Like McCarthy, he saw the censure attempt as part of some devious and dark conspiracy aimed at discrediting anti-communism — and so at destroying America. He named no names, but in the best

McCarthyite tradition he painted a picture of a vague and nebulous plot, colossal in its evil intent.

"Actually," he said, "those unknown engineers of censure hope that this will be the culminating act in the merciless fight to destroy a United States Senator and the fight against communism which has been crackling on a score of left-wing fronts for over four years.

"What kind of fight has it been? It has been a fight which has been laden with hypocrisy. The masterminds of this fight have said one thing and have meant another . . .

"All of the discredited and embittered figures of the Hiss-Yalta period of American dishonor have crawled out from under their logs to join the efforts to get even. The news columns and the airways have been filled with their talk about 'civil liberties,' 'ethical codes,' and 'protection of the innocent' while these people have dipped in the smut pot to discredit Senator McCarthy and his work against communism."

Goldwater charged that "extremely important men" had "vowed to drive McCarthy from a position of influence in this country." Just who were these men? Goldwater did not say. Just how did he know that such a conspiracy actually existed? Goldwater did not say. In the lexicon of the Radical Right, in which he was rapidly becoming more adept, it is not necessary to establish facts or to prove charges; it is necessary only to make them in a style so sweeping and emotional that it triggers the adrenalin and blanks out the need to think.

Goldwater's denunciation of the forces of evil that were in league against the hero of the witch-hunt triggered a wave of applause in the packed galleries, but it could not change the mood of the Senate. Senators who had countenanced all of McCarthy's other antics and had walked in almost psychopathic fear of his vitriolic tongue could not bring themselves to blink at his offense in calling one of their own a human phenomenon "without brains or guts." Goldwater recognized this and suggested that McCarthy apologize to Senators Hendrickson and Watkins for the harsh things he had said about them. In Goldwater's code, this is the way a gentleman should act after performing an ungentlemanly deed, but McCarthy was not Goldwater's kind of a gentleman. He wouldn't yield an inch. Goldwater's attempt to talk reason to his friend — and he made a determined attempt — collapsed before McCarthy's angry, bellowed refusal, and McCarthy pursued his headstrong way to the inevitable end, a 67-22 vote of censure, with only Republicans, Goldwater foremost among them, opposing the verdict.

Was Goldwater's stand on the key issue of McCarthyism prompted only by partisan considerations? Or did it represent his own deep-felt, strongly held convictions? There can be no doubt it represented the latter.

In the course of his speech, it is true, Goldwater had deplored "the spectacle of cannibalism" that he perceived in the Republican Party "busily chewing on itself." Goldwater has always felt that Republicans should not war with each other, but should unite against the enemy. However, his feelings on the McCarthy issue ran much deeper than that. There was a mental kinship between the two men, as has been demonstrated time and time again by some of Goldwater's own performances and utterances.

Eisenhower may not have had the fortitude to speak out against McCarthy and others of his ilk, but he felt a deep personal repugnance toward such "reckless vilifiers." When Senator William E. Jenner, of Indiana, another Republican of the McCarthy stripe and a traducer of General Marshall, embraced him on a public platform, Ike reacted with deep aversion and told Emmet Hughes: "I felt dirty from the touch of the man." No such feeling of uncleanliness from close association rubbed off on Goldwater. On the contrary, in an appearance on the American Forum of the Air on Nov. 29, 1953, Goldwater declared:

"Those people who would like to do away with McCarthy, Velde or Jenner would be the type of people who would also like to coddle communism. Now, if they want to do that, then the thing to do is to defeat those men in the coming election or to defeat the party so that the chairman might be changed. Do I stick up for McCarthy, do you say? Yes, I have always done it and I intend to continue."

This was thinking right in line with the anti-anti-anti-Communist idiocy that was to take such strong root in Phoenix. No one could oppose the ranters and ravers of anti-Communism without being branded as a Communist stooge or dupe, or someone who wanted to "coddle communism." There was no room for principle.

Even after McCarthy's sudden death, which came not long after the Senate censure and the Republican disaster in the Congressional elections of 1954, Goldwater continued to speak with passion about his fallen friend and hero. He waxed most eloquent on the subject in a eulogy to McCarthy delivered on June 8, 1957 before the Wisconsin Republican State Convention.

"Joe and I became friends long before either of us entered the Senate . . . ," he said. "During the time that I had the good fortune to serve with him in the Senate, I've found further evidence of his distinction as a Senator, as a Republican and as a friend. He was a faithful, tireless and conscientious American. He fought just as hard for the things he believed were right as he did against the things he knew were wrong.

"Joe McCarthy gave himself — his life — to the service of his God and his country. . . . He was completely selfless and his single motive was the preservation of those principles which make it possible for the Republican Party to proclaim now its fulfillment of the confidence of all Americans.

"Because Joe McCarthy lived, we are a safer, freer, more vigilant nation today. That fact, even though he no longer dwells among us, will never perish. And I know you will join with me in thanking God that while Joe lived he made a contribution to his countrymen that will forever redound to the credit of the people of Wisconsin and to your Republican organization."

Goldwater apparently actually believed it — and has never ceased to believe it. In 1961, when Irwin Ross, of *The New York Post*, interviewed him, he was still defending McCarthy. Goldwater conceded that McCarthy "at times went off half-cocked or not cocked at all," but he argued defensively: "I never was convinced that Joe McCarthy had done great damage to the country." When Ross mentioned McCarthy's "calamitous impact" on the morale of the State Department and the foreign service, Goldwater insisted: "I've never noticed it in my travels." He concluded: "I can't find any concrete evidence that this thing called McCarthyism upset the people of the country. Joe was well-received by the man in the street."

Barry Goldwater was himself not above indulging in a lashing, McCarthyite kind of innuendo. Typical was the incident of Alan Barth, an editorial writer for the *Washington Post* and a writer generally respected in the profession. Barth wrote an article for the March, 1954, issue of *Harper's* entitled "How Good Is an FBI Report?" It questioned the methods used by J. Edgar Hoover's Federal Bureau of Investigation in preparing confidential personnel reports for the guidance of government officials. To intimate that Hoover and the FBI are less than perfect is the cardinal sin in the precincts of the Radical Right, and Barry Goldwater promptly saw Red.

Taking the Senate floor, he denounced this "smear of the FBI," and then he proceeded to demonstrate how a good smear is handled.

"For years," he thundered, "Barth has denounced loyalty programs, and his heart has bled for Communists, their stooges, spies, and persons whose acts were akin to treason."

There was more in the same vein, so much more that George C. Connelly was later impelled to write in the *Berkshire Eagle* in Pittsfield, Mass.:

"Because he said this on the floor of the Senate he could not be sued. He is not above McCarthy tactics. Barth, he told the Senate, wrote an article back in 1946 critical of the House Un-American Activities committee for a magazine published by a man who was a director of the Joint Anti-Fascist Committee which was on the Attorney General's list. This is certainly shaking the hand that shook the hand of Joseph R. McCarthy."

Goldwater's friends profess to be amazed that the Barth incident should have left such a residue of bitterness. They point out that, before Goldwater denounced Barth on the floor, he did the gallant and gentlemanly thing by telephoning Barth and advising him in advance that the attack was to be made.

The Barth incident was by no means an isolated one. Goldwater has not joined the John Birch Society in advocating that Chief Justice Earl Warren should be impeached — or hanged, the method of retribution openly advocated by some other Radical Rightists. But his view of Warren is essentially the view of the ranting extremists. In September, 1953, President Eisenhower told a White House luncheon, at which Goldwater was a guest, that he intended to appoint Warren Chief Justice. Goldwater promptly told the President he didn't like the idea. Recalling the incident with evident satisfaction in a speech in Jackson, Mississippi, on April 17, 1959, Goldwater said he had told Ike that Warren was unqualified "because he hasn't practiced law in twenty-five years, has never been a Judge and is a Socialist."

In a series of speeches in 1955 and 1956, Goldwater hewed closely to the McCarthy line. In a speech to the Women's Republican Club of the 13th Congressional District in Chicago in mid-February, 1955, he charged that the Democrats had let Communists and their sympathizers into the federal government — and then had protected them after they got there, partly because they were afraid of arousing the wrath of the Soviets and partly because they feared exposure might blow the Democratic Party "sky high." In a speech in Phoenix in early May, 1956, he declared that Harry Truman was "the architect of everything that is wrong with America today." He added: "A sound defeat this year will help the Democratic Party to wave again the flag of true patriotism and Americanism. . ." Obviously, the Democrats were still badly steeped in treason.

Sometimes Goldwater, whose attractive personality seems to provide cover for his deeds as McCarthy's did not, becomes so extreme that he cuts a positively ridiculous figure. One of his most ludicrous performances was staged on November 26, 1960 when he spoke at the National Interfraternity Conference at Los Angeles. Here he seriously advanced the proposition that the college fraternities were the nation's first line of defense against communism. "Where fraternities are not allowed, communism flourishes," he proclaimed. The reference was unmistakable. Harvard University, long regarded by fanatics as the intellectual seedbed of radicalism, has no fraternities. "Young men who are inexperienced but have faith are more useful than older, experienced men without faith," Goldwater thundered on. "And we look more and more to fraternities to provide our future." The fraternity system, he solemnly assured his audience, was "a bastion of American strength."

Harvard students responded by sending Goldwater an 18-inch fraternity paddle. They informed him they had organized Iota Beta Phi (Inexperienced But Faithful) and wrote: "We send you this paddle to symbolize your election to the post of honorable grand wizard of the IBP and because we regard it as the best means to your end."

The fraternity episode was not the only McCarthyite foray by Goldwater in the educational field. In an editorial on June 17, 1961, the Providence *Journal* took Goldwater to task for another, similar performance. In addressing the Senate Education sub-committee, Goldwater had called for the retention of the loyalty oath and non-communist affidavits from students seeking government loans under the National Defense Education Act. In doing so, he listed thirty-seven colleges that, he said, had campus chapters of the Fair Play for Cuba Committee. He then emphasized that the presidents or trustees of these same thirty-seven colleges had opposed the loyalty oath and non-communist affidavits. The implication was the familiar one — that the stand the colleges had taken was the result of some devious communist plot. Since Brown University was one of the institutions on Goldwater's suspect list, the Providence *Journal* took up the cudgels. "This is precisely the sort of specious reasoning, flimsy analogy and accusation by innuendo that reached a peak of popularity during the period of McCarthyism," it wrote. "It is just as distasteful now as it was then."

The *Journal* pointed out that "many of our most distinguished colleges and universities" were refusing to participate in the student loan program as long as non-communist affidavits were required. It emphasized that there were valid grounds for such objections, and it stressed these points: that the affidavits represented an invasion of belief; that students were placed in a special category because no such affidavits were required of others receiving government loans and grants; and that the oath was utterly useless anyway because the dedicated Communist wouldn't hesitate to sign such affidavits.

The irresponsibility with which Goldwater makes such charges — passion-arousing accusations that set the saliva running in the glands of the Radical Right — was perhaps best illustrated by his performance of November 13, 1962 when he swung a McCarthyite haymaker at Adlai Stevenson in a speech before the Wings Club in New York. Goldwater called for the dismissal of Stevenson as U. N. Ambassador because he had "consistently urged a soft policy toward communism, both in Cuba and elsewhere throughout the world."

Goldwater included in his attack Chester Bowles, Arthur Schlesinger Jr., and Richard Goodwin. He said, being a gentleman, that he had "no doubts" about their loyalty, but "they just don't understand communism and the modern world."

"I am more concerned over a civilian like Adlai Stevenson telling the United Nations that we are prepared to take 'risks' to lessen the chance of an intensified arms race with Russia than I am about military men who regard the Soviets as an implacable foe which will never deal in honor," he said.

The reference to "risks," it developed, was a complete distortion of a speech Stevenson had delivered in the U. N. Stevenson quickly pointed out that, in appealing for agreements to slow down the arms race, he had specifically and categorically said the United States did *not* intend to stake its existence or risk its survival on "blind trust." The language he had used was so specific it left no doubt, and Goldwater's intemperate charge backfired against its author.

Former President Eisenhower came to Stevenson's assistance and rebuked Goldwater. The Arizona *Journal* commented that Goldwater obviously was opposed to any "risk" in slowing down the arms race, and it added: "We would like to see him accept the possibility of peace with as open a mind as he accepts the possibility of war." In Chicago, the *Sun-Times* denounced Goldwater for applying the "soft on communism" label to Stevenson. "It is a 'smear' term, one which, perhaps, can be safely employed in derogation without risking suit for libel or slander," the *Sun Times* wrote. And the Chicago *Daily News* added: "The distortion of Goldwater's lifting the phrase (risk) from its context is obvious. We must also conclude it was deliberate." Goldwater's tactics in this instance, the paper commented, were akin to "the smear tactics so dear to the Communists themselves."

Such incidents amply illustrate a cast of mind and method that, despite Goldwater's distinguished appearance and facile charm, places him ideologically in the brotherhood of fanatics.

CHAPTER X

On the Labor Trail

The years 1957 and 1958 marked Goldwater's emergence into the national limelight. He had attracted notice previously with his defense of McCarthy and his widely discussed fantasy that "labor goons" were about to take over the Democratic Party. These stands had given his name considerable currency beyond the confines of Arizona, but it took the events of 1957 and 1958 to lay the foundation for his reputation as the nation's "Mr. Conservative."

Two issues were primarily responsible for the building of the image — Goldwater's attack on the high Eisenhower budgets and Goldwater's attack on Walter Reuther and the citadels of organized labor.

The first stand, which saw the Senator from Arizona excoriate the leadership of his own party, marked him as the outstanding advocate of the balanced budget and the so-called doctrine of fiscal integrity, faiths that long had been cornerstones of conservative Republicanism; and the second made business leaders feel that they had at last found a personable champion to combat what they regarded as the dark and menacing forces of labor.

The battle over the budget erupted in April, 1957. Eisenhower, who had campaigned on a platform calling for a reduction of federal expenditures and a balanced budget, sent to Congress a fiscal program that all but carpeted the aisles with conservatives felled by apoplexy. It called for expenditures of $71.8 billion. Though the federal budget would soar in a few years to the $100 billion level, this was at the time the highest peacetime budget a President had ever submitted. Goldwater was shocked.

On April 8, 1957 he took the floor in the Senate and, using the budget as a springboard, denounced the Eisenhower administration and ridiculed Ike's entire concept of a "new" and "modern" Republicanism. The budget, Goldwater said acidly, was a "betrayal of the people's trust." It was, he said, "with the deepest sorrow that I must pass such a judgment on my own President." But, he added, he could not help it. The budget "not only shocks me, but it weakens my faith in the constant assurances we have received from the Administration that its aim was to cut spending, balance the budget, reduce the national debt, cut taxes . . ."

In scathing reference to Ike's "modern Republicanism," he continued:

"Indeed, it is curious that the Administration's departure from its pledges to the American people should occur during what I believe will be the rather brief tenure of this splinterized concept of Republican philosophy."

If the budget were not cut drastically, Goldwater warned, "there will be a lot of people on both sides of the aisle . . . who will not be here two years from now." And he wondered aloud, like a man considering the possibility of some devious conspiracy, "what strange magic" had changed the President from the Ike who had campaigned for economy in 1952.

President Eisenhower, in a news conference on April 14, was asked about the criticisms of his massive budget, and in what sounded to newsmen like a direct slap at Goldwater, he retorted that the GOP had to face up to "the needs of the people today, not 1860."

This relegation of Goldwater to the previous century stung the Arizona Senator. The very next day, he took the Senate floor to renew his attack on the administration and on what he called Ike's "splinterized concept" of "modern Republicanism."

Everybody agreed, Goldwater said, that the problems of 1957 weren't the problems of 1860, but the trouble was that the administration should "quit looking for things to do for the people." This, he said, was what was running up the cost of government; and the administration, by advocating extra adventures in the welfare field, was creating its own fiscal problems. "I find no widespread demand, for instance," Goldwater said, "for federal aid to education, health insurance or even for expanded minimum wage coverage."

In budgets of the Cold War era, military expenditures generally account for some 75 percent of the total. The amount of money spent on welfare programs has been comparatively miniscule, and hard arithmetic says that no budget is going to be drastically reduced or balanced unless military hardware and its allied items are slashed. This, of course, would be anathema to Goldwater, a man who always advocates a harder, tougher line and more reliance on military strength, even if it leads to war. The intellectual incapacity of Goldwater to banish the myths in which he believes and come to grips with reality is demonstrated in such inescapable conflicts between the separate wings of the programs he advocates.

The scrap over the Eisenhower budget of 1957 faded gradually into history. Since Congress was on the whole as military minded as Goldwater, there wasn't much it could do to cut back the swelling tide of federal expenditures. The controversy in the long run accomplished little, but it had served to furbish Goldwater's conservative image with people of like mind.

More dramatic and more enduring were the effects of Goldwater's war on Walter Reuther. This was conducted like a blood feud; and though Goldwater has never been able to pin anything discreditable on Reuther, he still keeps trying and he still views the UAW chief as a major menace to the republic.

The background of this vendetta is decidedly odd, to say the least. Goldwater himself confesses that he had only the scantiest knowledge of labor problems when Taft named him to the Labor Committee. As head of the Goldwater department store, he had had no union problems. Organizers had come in a couple of times, Goldwater says, and he'd always told them to go ahead if they wanted to — but to do their organizing on their own time and the workers', not on the store's. After a couple of days, the organizers would return and confess their failure. Goldwater was paying higher wages and benefits than the union had won elsewhere, he says, and the union had nothing to offer. This marked the extent of Goldwater's personal contact with the problems of union relations until the eve of his election to the Senate.

The campaign of 1952, however, was to be the medium for his making a strange contact. Despite the contributions of H. L. Hunt and other Texas oil magnates, campaign finances were, as they always are, something of a problem, and so Goldwater was highly pleased when, one day in the heat of the fray, an uncle of his wife's came in with a check for $500 from a man named William Nelson. After the victory over McFarland, the uncle suggested that it would be fitting for Goldwater to express his gratitude for such a handsome donation. Goldwater agreed, autographed a picture of himself, and gave it to the uncle for delivery to William Nelson.

A couple of days later, a man whom Goldwater had never seen before walked into his office.

"Don't you know who I am?" the man said.

Goldwater said that he didn't.

"I'm Bill Nelson," the man said. "But that isn't my real name. I'm really Willie Bioff."

He took out the autographed picture Goldwater had sent him, slowly tore it up and dropped the pieces into the wastebasket.

"You don't want that thing floating around to embarrass you now that you're a Senator," he said.

Goldwater was soon to realize just how embarrassing it might have been if his autographed picture had been found in the possession of Willie Bioff. For Bioff was indeed notorious. Back in the late thirties, he and his partner, George Browne, operating from their posts as union officials, had set up a shakedown and extortion racket that had mulcted the movie industry of Hollywood of literally millions of dollars. Their six-year reign of terror had come to an end in 1941 when a federal grand jury in New York had indicted them for violations of the federal anti-racketeering statutes. Bioff and Browne had been convicted and packed away in prison for long terms; there they had turned informers and had given the government information that enabled it to prosecute high members of the Chicago mob who had been their partners in the extortion racket. Bioff, rewarded for his services and released on parole, had settled in Phoenix and adopted the name of William Nelson.

Such was the history of the man who had donated $500 to Barry Goldwater's first Senatorial campaign. He had been a panderer, extortionist and stool pigeon. He reeked of an unsavory past. Yet Goldwater admittedly wasn't revolted. He talked companionably with Willie Bioff, and he even came, in some odd way, to develop an affection for this stocky racketeer with the checkered past.

"He was a pleasant guy," Goldwater told Irwin Ross in 1961, in trying to explain this weird relationship. "He didn't look like a bum or talk like one. You had to forget his early background, that he was a pimp and so on. He was well regarded in town. He had a nice little house, quite a sizable art collection."

During the next three years, Willie Bioff and Senator Barry Goldwater saw a lot of each other. Goldwater admitted to Irwin Ross that he tried to be discreet about the relationship, but he found Bioff a fascinating character, loaded with all kinds of lore about crooked unions and the way they operated. Westbrook Pegler, who was privy to Goldwater confidences, was fully aware of the friendship and later explained it this way: "Bioff educated Goldwater in the practical, coercive, terroristic and often criminal methods of union bosses . . . He concentrated on Walter Reuther and (James R.) Hoffa (boss of the powerful Teamsters union)." Ross speculated that Goldwater's deep-seated animus against Walter Reuther may have stemmed from this indoctrination by Willie Bioff.

Other accounts would indicate that the Bioff-Goldwater comradeship may have been less discreet and far more intimate than Goldwater now contends. Ed Reid and Ovid Demaris, in *The Green Felt Jungle*, their best-selling exposé of the Las Vegas rackets, wrote that in 1955 the two men were often seen together and that Goldwater "personally chauffeured Bioff in his private plane all over the Southwest to attend various parties. When questioned by reporters, Goldwater became indignant, protesting that he had no idea that his friend, one William Nelson, was the notorious Willie Bioff. Later, the Senator changed his story. Bioff, he said, was helping him in his study of American labor, giving him a special insight into union racketeering."

Another Goldwater associate during this period, according to Reid and Demaris, was Gus Greenbaum, a Phoenix gambler with high underworld ties, long a power in Las Vegas, and onetime Mayor of Paradise, the area of "the Strip." Greenbaum had taken over the flamboyant Flamingo after Buggsy Siegel had been liquidated for pouring millions of the mob's money down this expensive rat hole. In one year, Greenbaum had wiped out the red ink and had the Flamingo paying off in millions. Later he had tried to retire to Phoenix, but the mob got into multi-million-dollar trouble with the new Riviera and served Greenbaum with an ultimatum to come back to Las Vegas and bail them out. Greenbaum knew better than to defy the ukase and assumed management of the Riviera. But he took along with him a man who had become his almost inseparable shadow — Willie Bioff. And he gave Willie full charge of entertainment at the Riviera.

High mobsters who had been double-crossed by Bioff in the old days were not enchanted by Greenbaum's choice of companions. They told him to "get rid of the fink or else," but this time Gus Greenbaum didn't listen.

Barry Goldwater, according to Reid and Demaris, was also on a friendly basis with Gus Greenbaum. They put it this way:

"Along the Strip in Las Vegas, Barry Goldwater is known by the wags and older show girls as a real 'swinger.' His brother, Robert (Bobby), is a Gold Card holder and one of the 'high rollers.' Bobby still gambles regularly in Las Vegas, but the Senator, since Greenbaum's death and his own personal 'high hopes,' has steered clear of the town except for brief visits.

"In the old days, when Gus was Mayor of Paradise, Barry Goldwater was a frequent visitor, occupying plush suites, first at the Flamingo and then later (when Gus changed his operation) at the Riviera. Some of the Senator's speeches were written in Las Vegas. The authors know of at least one occasion, in 1955, when Greenbaum's ghost writer helped the Senator with one of his speeches."

The year 1955 marked the end of these relationships — and in decidedly violent fashion. On the morning of November 4, 1955, Willie Bioff walked out of his Phoenix home, got into his car and threw on the ignition switch. An instantaneous blast from a dynamite bomb wired to the ignition system blew the car and Willie to bits.

Police in their investigation learned that on his last trip to Las Vegas some two weeks before, Bioff had been flown back to Phoenix by Barry Goldwater in his private plane. According to Goldwater, this is the only time he ever flew Bioff anywhere, and it happened entirely by accident. He and his wife, Peggy, had flown into Las Vegas, where he addressed the American Mining Congress. Mrs. Goldwater, who never has liked flying and who dreaded the return trip at night over the mountains in a small plane, had planned to take a commercial airliner home. At the airport, she encountered Willie Bioff and his wife, who were going back to Phoenix on the same airliner. The plane, however, developed engine trouble and never did get off the apron. The three travelers were stranded. So Goldwater bundled them all into his plane and flew them to Phoenix.

Realizing that a distorted version of the incident might get out and do him harm, Goldwater promptly confided all to Westbrook Pegler. When Bioff violently departed from this life a few weeks later, Pegler suggested that "union bosses" had had him bumped off because he had been tutoring Goldwater about their methods of operation.

There never was any evidence to support this Pegler rationale. Indeed, what tracks there were pointed to the Mafia rather than to "union bosses." Bioff's demise had its effect on Greenbaum, who gradually went to pot, living high on heroin and whores. The mob decided that he had become an unreliable custodian of some of its most precious secrets, and so the end came on December 3, 1958. On that day a housekeeper found Gus Greenbaum and his wife in their Phoenix home, dead with their throats slashed. Among the mourners at the funeral, according to Reid and Demaris, was Senator Barry Goldwater.

Such was Barry Goldwater's private background briefing in the intricacies of the labor movement. Few would have considered Willie Bioff the best and most unbiased of tutors, but Goldwater by his own account evidently felt satisfied he was getting from Bioff the inside dope about what really goes on in labor. According to the Goldwater-Pegler version of this weird relationship, Bioff aimed his shafts at both Walter Reuther and James R. Hoffa; but only the innuendo against Reuther really took root and fertilized in the brain of Barry Goldwater. There are many (Robert Kennedy foremost among them) who would consider Hoffa the more ruthless and unscrupulous labor boss, but Goldwater has never been able to put his heart into a Hoffa vendetta. Only Reuther is his chosen black beast in the labor jungle. This is most curious. It leads inevitably to the speculation that Goldwater's opposition to Reuther is based not so much on high principle as on arch-conservative fear, for Reuther indubitably has been the most successful architect of labor participation in politics, and poses the most direct threat to the kind of nineteenth-century conservatism that Barry Goldwater espouses.

Conviction is conveyed by one of the more revealing exchanges of the McClellan Committee hearings into labor rackets. The committee, on which Goldwater was the leading Republican member, earlier had exposed the peculations and misdeeds of Teamster boss Dave Beck in a headline scandal that had rocked the nation, and now it had on the stand, in this August of 1957, the short, burly, hard-faced leader who had picked up the reins dropping from Beck's palsied hands — James Riddle Hoffa. The junior Senator from Arizona was questioning Hoffa.

He had brought out, in most gentlemanly questioning, the dangers implicit in Hoffa's plan to form an over-all transportation union including truckers, airline personnel, longshoremen and transit workers. Goldwater wondered mildly whether such a colossus, in the hands of one man, might not give that man such power that he would become a menace to the nation, and then in a long, rambling question he made it crystal clear just what kind of a threat most concerned him.

"Now," said Goldwater to Hoffa, "whether or not you or any other labor leader ever used that monopoly to the disadvantage of the country would be up to you. If you use that monopoly at the bargaining table, that is one thing. But to use it to advance a political theory is entirely another thing. I think that actually talking about it now, extending this kind of conversation to include all labor leaders, and government, we possibly can come up with the answer in the form of legislation that will prevent things happening that you do not want to have happen and I do not want to have happen. We both recognize that it can happen."

Hoffa immediately picked up the cue. He told Goldwater that "when you separate the political from the economic, you and I could have a different discussion." Labor leaders, he said, had no business trying to influence politics. Goldwater was obviously delighted with this fine expression of high principle. He reminded his partner in this surprising mental rapport that there were other labor leaders in the country — men not at all friendly to Hoffa, at that — who held different thoughts about labor's participation in politics. Could Hoffa see what dangers might arise if such men took over a union like the huge transportation union he was going to form?

Hoffa could see the danger, all right. "Maybe better than you can, Senator," he told Goldwater.

"I am . . . glad to hear you say that," Goldwater told him.

With this encouragement, Hoffa expanded upon the desperate lengths to which *some* labor leaders would go to extend their influence into politics. Hoffa wanted no part of this, he said. He wouldn't want anyone telling *him* what candidate he should support. Goldwater was gratified by these fine sentiments, and he wiped away the pretext that they were talking about "some labor leaders." It was really just one — Walter Reuther. This was the exchange:

GOLDWATER: Well, Mr. Hoffa, just to wind this up, I think we both recognize that in the writing in the clouds today there is an individual who would like to see that happen in this country. I do not like to ever suggest to let you and him fight, but for the good of the labor movement I am very hopeful that your philosophy prevails.

HOFFA: I assure you that the American people will accept my philosophy and not the one of the other.

Later, of course, it became even less popular to side with Jimmy Hoffa, and Goldwater, dogged by his happy reflection that "I am very hopeful that your philosophy prevails," has been driven into repeated explanations. It was, he has said, only a chance remark, a response to Hoffa's declaration that unions should keep out of politics. And, anyway, Goldwater argues, Hoffa later made the whole exchange meaningless by indulging in political activities himself.

The length of the colloquy between Hoffa and Goldwater is in itself proof that both men knew what they were doing and precisely where they were headed. The words of the record convey the spirit of their fraternity; but, according to some newsmen who witnessed the scene, no dust-dry transcript can do full justice to the warmth of their manner. John Herling, columnist of *The Washington Daily News*, later wrote that no one who had witnessed the surprising scene could ever forget "that gentle examination of the Teamsters leader by Sen. Goldwater." Goldwater, he said, had brought Hoffa "succor . . . across the desert sands. With simple, effortless charm, Sen. Goldwater pressed the cup of hope to the parched Hoffa lips." One after-effect, Herling wrote in another column, was that Goldwater and Hoffa quietly collaborated in some extracurricular activity designed to accomplish their mutual objective — the downfall of Walter Reuther.

"In Michigan," Herling wrote, "Mr. Hoffa's wide circles of influence have happily provided Sen. Goldwater's investigators — notably John J. McGovern — with a groaning smorgasbord of fact and fancy on the Reuther career. Many of the McGovern informants include Mr. Reuther's enemies in the union and management field with weird lacings of underworld types and their legal mouthpieces."

It was this, Herling wrote, that inspired Goldwater to demand in stentorian tones that the McClellan committee investigate Reuther and all his works. Voicing his demand on the floor of the Senate, Goldwater intoned: "Let Reuther stand up against the truth as it will be developed in these hearings. As for myself, I would rather have Jimmy Hoffa stealing my money than Walter Reuther stealing my freedom."

Goldwater clamored for Reuther hearings, not just on the

floor of the Senate, but in an unceasing drumfire of public denunciations that he delivered, quite literally, from one end of the country to the other. He gave the impression of a man who was positively hipped on a very special antagonism. Speaking at a Salute-to-Eisenhower dinner in Detroit in January, 1957, he called Reuther "the most dangerous man in America." At the close of his speech, finding he had a few minutes left to fill, he returned to Reuther again, with the preoccupation of a dog who cannot leave a tasty bone alone. And this time he really blasted from the hip, calling Reuther "more dangerous than the Sputniks or anything Russia might do."

Reuther, short, red-haired and bouncy, possessed of one of the fastest minds and quickest tongues in America, wasn't the man to take this McCarthyite slur lying down. Three days later, at a UAW convention, he repaid Goldwater in coin of equal weight, minted in vitriol. The Senator, he said, was "this country's No. 1 political fanatic, its No. 1 anti-labor baiter, its No. 1 peddler of class hatred." He added, for good measure, that Goldwater was "mentally unbalanced and needs a psychiatrist."

This was getting rough, even for Goldwater and Reuther. Later, reflecting about his Sputnik crack, Goldwater concluded in his gentlemanly way that he was sorry he had made it. "There are words of mine floating around in the ether that I would like to reach up and eat," he said. But he simply could not refrain, almost every time he opened his mouth, from putting more words up in the ether that should have been eaten. He appeared constitutionally unable to divorce himself from the sniping that seemed as involuntary as a reflex with him every time Reuther's name was mentioned.

His favorite fantasy was that Reuther would destroy democratic government and take over the country. Speaking before the Board of Trade on May 8, 1957, Goldwater denounced Reuther's "one-man rule" and proclaimed: "A check must be put on him quickly. If it isn't, he and the men around him will socialize the United States." In another speech in Phoenix, and in still another in Saginaw, Michigan, he blamed Reuther for having brought the state of Michigan "to the verge of bankruptcy." All of this was grist for the journalistic mill, and the Reuther-Goldwater feud made headlines across the nation.

Goldwater's persistent intemperance where Reuther was concerned was perhaps most vividly demonstrated in an appearance on *Meet the Press* on September 1, 1957, months after he had had a chance to reflect and regret his Sputnik remark. Edwin Lahey, of the Chicago *Daily News,* was doing the questioning, and this was the sequence:

LAHEY: Senator, you and Jimmy Hoffa share the belief, I believe, that the world would have been better off if Walter Reuther had never got out of Wheeling, West Virginia.

GOLDWATER: No, if he'd stayed in Russia.

LAHEY: A lot of people think that Reuther in the last twenty years has made some kind of contribution to the family life of the automobile workers. I'd like to hear you say what you don't like about Reuther.

GOLDWATER: I can't argue that he hasn't made a contribution to the life of the working people in his union because it's quite obvious that he has. I don't trust Mr. Reuther because of his socialist belief . . .

Marquis Childs, of the St. Louis *Post-Dispatch,* pointed out that, in his 1952 campaign, Goldwater had had heavy financial support from major oil interests and from firms that had had trouble with Reuther's UAW. Goldwater acknowledged he had received a "rather small" contribution from Borg-Warner, the auto parts firm organized by his wife's father, and he admitted that he had been an ardent advocate of the tidelands oil bill so much desired by the oil interests. But he said he had been speaking for this "ever since I can remember" and the campaign contributions had not influenced his stand.

Lawrence E. Spivak thought that Goldwater's Russian crack about Reuther shouldn't be ignored and said it should be pointed out, in all fairness, that Reuther wasn't born in Russia, he'd merely gone there on a visit. Goldwater said he had been speaking "facetiously," but then he compounded his previous felony by adding, "I thought with his beliefs he might be happier over there." This was too much for Peter Edson, who asked:

"Senator, don't you give Walter Reuther credit for having conducted a pretty good campaign to drive communism out of the labor movement?"

"Well, yes, when he finally got started on it he did all right . . .," Goldwater acknowledged.

The record on this point was indisputable. Walter Reuther had been one of the first major labor leaders in the nation to become concerned about communistic influences in the labor movement; he had begun his battle to drive the Communists out of positions of influence in the UAW immediately after the war; and he had finally won after a knock-down, drag-out brawl that lasted through most of 1946 and 1947. The record was incontestable, but obviously it stuck in Goldwater's throat to acknowledge it. He preferred by innuendo to continue painting Reuther Red.

It was against this background that Goldwater forced his investigation of Walter Reuther and the UAW. Robert F. Kennedy, who was counsel to the McClellan Committee, has given a graphic account of the dirty in-fighting that preceded the probe in his best-selling *The Enemy Within*. For months, Kennedy wrote, the press of the nation was filled with stories planted by the Republican committee members that the Kennedys, for political purposes, were blocking a much-needed investigation of Reuther and the UAW. The Republicans appeared convinced that the brutal, years-long, UAW-Kohler strike at Sheboygan, Wis., would furnish the ammunition to prove that Reuther was little better than an unprincipled thug. Though the strike had been thoroughly investigated twice previously without turning up any such information, Chairman John L. McClellan and Bobby Kennedy dispatched investigators to the scene to make a preliminary study. They reported back that they could find no new, damaging evidence. In spite of this, *Newsweek* magazine came out with a story it attributed to GOP committee members charging that the Kennedys were disregarding known evidence and protecting Reuther by blocking an investigation.

At the next meeting of the committee, Senator John F. Kennedy called for a showdown and publicly challenged the Republican Senators to produce the known facts if they had them. It was obvious they didn't. One and all, they denied they had ever said any such thing. They were completely satisfied, they said, with the way the investigation was being handled.

"So far as this Republican member is concerned, I'm as happy as a squirrel in a little cage," Goldwater proclaimed.

Senator Karl Mundt, this being a day for wild-life analogies, didn't think that any squirrel could be as happy as he was. "I too am perfectly happy and I'm as happy as a South Dakota pheasant in a South Dakota cornfield," he announced.

Evidently the squirrels of Arizona and the pheasants of South Dakota do not retain such ecstasy for long, for the Republican happiness boys had hardly proclaimed their delight before the planted stories began to appear in the press again, harping on the same theme — the Democrats were protecting Reuther.

Bobby Kennedy felt that these underhanded attacks were jeopardizing the committee's status. If public faith in its integrity should be undermined, all its work would go down the drain. Worried, he went to McClellan and proposed a plan; the Republicans should be given their own counsel — and a completely free hand — to "get" Reuther if they could. McClellan backed the idea.

". . . Some time before this," Bobby Kennedy wrote, "at Senator Goldwater's request, we had hired an investigator and assistant counsel, Jack McGovern, who had been the minority counsel for the Lobbying Committee. McGovern was a Republican and the only appointment made to the staff because of political considerations."

And so on July 22, 1957 McGovern was placed in full charge of the UAW-Kohler investigation.

Months passed, and finally, in October, 1957, McGovern submitted a preliminary report to Chairman McClellan. According to Bobby Kennedy, it turned out to be a digest of information elicited in a previous National Labor Relations Board investigation, with heavy stress put on every fact unfavorable to the UAW and all detail reflecting on the Kohler Company eliminated. Kennedy was distressed at the patent dishonesty of the presentation. During a committee hearing in November, 1957, he wrote, he sat off to one side and discussed the McGovern report with Goldwater.

"I told him how dishonest McGovern's report was, and that he would not remain on the committee staff if he were anybody but a political appointee," Kennedy wrote. "Senator Goldwater said he thought I should take over the UAW-Kohler investigation. I replied that under the circumstances because of the stories originating from the Committee's Republican Senators in the press, I was reluctant to do so. I told him our preliminary investigation had found the facts were essentially those disclosed in the NLRB report and therefore a new investigation was unlikely to accomplish what he wanted and expected, namely to destroy Walter Reuther. I told him I knew that if the investigations and hearings did not at least seriously tarnish Walter Reuther, there would be a charge of whitewash, and all the Committee's work would be affected.

"In the course of our talk Goldwater remarked that he was not interested in calling Reuther before the Committee, or even in investigating Reuther. For that matter, he said, he was not in favor of calling or investigating the UAW-Kohler dispute, either. I was surprised, but those days were full of surprises."

The reason for Goldwater's reluctance and the increasing reluctance of his Republican colleagues gradually became apparent. Even though they had been granted a free hand to run their own investigation of Reuther, they simply hadn't been able to dredge up the damning evidence that they had claimed must exist. With public hearings set for February and March, 1958, Bobby Kennedy became more and more concerned with the manner in which McGovern and Vern Johnson, a committee investigator, had conducted their research. A key witness whom Johnson was supposed to have questioned told Kennedy he had never been approached by anyone from the committee. When Kennedy had the committee's accountant examine the Kohler Company books, he found that McGovern and Johnson had neglected to report "large sums of money that the company had spent to purchase guns and ammunition shortly before the strike started. They also failed to tell us that the company officials held target practice at the plant just before the strike, using targets in the shape of human forms . . ."

All of these indications that the Republican committee members were running a vengeful and unprincipled probe boiled over on the eve of the committee hearings into what can only be described as a first-class scandal. Joseph Rauh, the scrappy Washington lawyer, came boiling into Kennedy's office. "He was angry because, he said, McGovern and Johnson had picked up a certain UAW official at eleven o'clock at night, driven him around and threatened to expose his alleged left-wing leanings if he did not turn informer on Walter Reuther," Kennedy wrote. "Rauh said the committee staff members had threatened and tried to blackmail the man. As chief counsel, what was I going to do about it?"

Kennedy called in McGovern and Johnson. They both denied the story. Johnson said he had questioned the UAW official in routine fashion, but had made no threats. McGovern denied ever interviewing the man or taking him on a midnight drive; he insisted the entire charge was false.

After the hearings started, UAW officials came back to Kennedy. They wanted the victim of the midnight browbeating sworn as a witness to tell his story from the stand. "I again went to McGovern," Kennedy wrote. "Again he denied that he had done any such thing. I told him the UAW was bringing the man in the next morning at ten-thirty o'clock and were going to demand that he testify. At nine-fifteen the following morning, McGovern came to my office. He told me he had lied. He said it would be very difficult for him if he were forced to admit publicly what he had done.

"I told him to get out of my office. I didn't want to have anything more to do with him . . ."

Kennedy, trying to protect the committee's name and reputation, got the UAW to agree — "but very reluctantly" — not to make the matter public at the time. But, as events were to show, nothing less than the public disclosure of fraud could have tempered the fanaticism with which the Republican members of the committee continued to pursue Reuther.

Their tactics were ruthless and uncompromising. Kohler Company witnesses were to be called in the pattern McGovern had mapped out, but the UAW wasn't to be given a similarly fair shake. The union wanted to lead off its side with Walter Reuther, but the Republican committee members wouldn't have it. They wanted to hear Reuther as late as possible, or not at all. Five executive sessions of the committee were devoted to this wrangle before McClellan finally yielded and let the Republicans have their way. The hearings began. "Never at any time during the five weeks of hearings did Senator Mundt, Senator Goldwater or Senator (Carl T.) Curtis [Goldwater's floor manager at the 1964 Republican convention] ask questions critical of the Kohler Company, or questions that would elicit a reply unfavorable to the company point of view," Kennedy wrote. "Apparently it never occurred to them that there were two sides to this controversy . . ."

Goldwater had demanded the "get-Reuther" probe and had been principally responsible for bringing it about. McGovern had been appointed as counsel to the Republican minority on the committee at his behest. And McGovern's conduct had been such it is difficult to see how a man of principle could have condoned it. McGovern had tried to browbeat a UAW witness and manufacture testimony; he had denied persistently that he had done this; he had admitted the truth only when threatened exposure forced a confession. Yet none of this weighed with Goldwater. Nothing tempered his tactics.

Bobby Kennedy later wrote:

"When it was brought out that there had been violence during the strike, Senator Goldwater observed that this was a pattern: the UAW had been part of the CIO, and more than thirty people had been killed in CIO strikes. The comment made a news story. What the Senator failed to mention was that *the thirty people who had been killed were all strikers.* Later on he followed this up by saying that the Communists used violence and it was significant that the CIO used similar tactics. My brother interrupted. He questioned whether there was any more significance in this fact than there was in the fact that we had a brother named Joe and Stalin's first name was also Joe." (Italics added.)

The climax to this farce (which was accepted as a high and principled crusade by much of the American press) came when the hearings were nearly over and a decision had to be made about what to do about Walter Reuther, who still had not been permitted to testify.

". . . On March 24," Kennedy wrote, "Senator Goldwater suddenly announced at a committee meeting that he saw no reason to call Walter Reuther; he did not believe Reuther could add anything, although if he did come he would have some questions to ask him.

"I thought Senator McClellan was going to faint at this. After all the charges of cover-up, whitewash and shielding, after months of investigation and weeks of hearings, Reuther's chief antagonist, Senator Goldwater, was suggesting that there was no reason to call him. When the Chairman recovered from his surprise, he said he would not be a party to denying Reuther an opportunity to testify . . ."

Reuther appeared at the end of March, and in a virtuoso performance, reduced the vendetta against him to a ridiculous shambles. This was the almost unanimous verdict of observers. One of the most vivid descriptions of Reuther in action was written by William V. Shannon, columnist of the New York *Post*. Shannon put it this way:

"'So I asked myself, what's wrong up in Sheboygan?'

"Having talked his standing-room-only audience glassy-eyed for 40 minutes on the dangers of communism, the United Automobile Workers' fight against gangsterism and the tragedy of human corruption, the witness had at last arrived, so to speak, in Sheboygan which put him in the geographical vicinity of the Kohler strike.

"It was the third act of the play, but something had gone awry. Director Barry Goldwater had lost control of the action, nobody could find the authorized script, and Walter Reuther, stage center and talking fast, was making up his lines as he went along . . . .

"Barry Goldwater is the first member of the Senate to fly a jet airplane, but cracking the sound barrier is child's play compared to trying to out-argue Walter Reuther. The solemn desert Don Quixote very soon had to take refuge in his dignity and remind the witness that it is the Senators who ask the questions.

"'Some day you and I are going to get together and lock horns,' Goldwater said, as if by way of offering consolation.

"'We're together here right now,' Reuther cracked back.

"The spectators applauded enthusiastically, but Goldwater demurred.

"John McClellan was not present for this ultimate humiliation. The reversal of roles between the Senator and the witness, this outrageous upstaging by Reuther, this virtuoso display of gesture, rhetoric and passion by a mere trade unionist not a member of the Senatorial guild, had saddened his heart and curled his nostrils. Sniffing disdainfully, McClellan had departed moments before, leaving to acting Chairman Ives the dim honor of presiding over the shambles produced by Ives' colleagues from the desert and the prairie. Why, he doubtless asked himself, do the Republicans always send us stock-company amateurs to do this professional work?"

Bobby Kennedy later wrote that, as Reuther was finishing his testimony, Goldwater "admitted to me: 'You were right. We never should have gotten into this matter. This investigation was not one in which we should have become involved.'"

A year later, just after the McClellan hearings had wound up, Kennedy was shocked to hear that Goldwater had given the press a statement accusing Kennedy of "having run out on the Reuther investigation." Kennedy wrote that he was "more disgusted than angry," and he kept telephoning Goldwater until he finally got him. He asked Goldwater whether he had, "in fact, made such a statement."

The rest of it, according to Kennedy — and Goldwater has never denied it — went this way:

"He said that was not exactly how he had expressed it, though he was not completely satisfied with what had been done in the case. I asked if there was anything further he thought I should do.

"'No, no,' he protested, 'I want to get back to Arizona now. I don't want any more hearings.'

"'Then why did you say it?' I asked.

"'That's politics,' he said."

It may be politics the way Barry Goldwater plays it, but,

clearly, under these circumstances, the game has little relation to principle or truth.

So flimsy indeed is the factual basis for Goldwater's anti-Reuther fixation that Goldwater himself, when driven into a corner, has to admit that he has never been able to get anything on Walter Reuther, not even with all the power of a U.S. Senator and the McClellan Committee behind him. But this still doesn't deter him from campaigning against Reuther as if Reuther were the devil himself.

This war of Goldwater fancy with established fact has led at times to acute, but momentary, embarrassments. One such fleeting moment of trial occurred April 2, 1961 on the CBS television program, *Washington Conversation*. Goldwater's derogatory references to Reuther led Paul Niven, the interviewer, to put this question:

"Is it fair to say that most of the corruption has been in the conservative unions of the old craft tradition, and that the industrial unions, like Mr. Reuther's . . . however dangerous their power may be, have been relatively clean in their administration of their finances?"

"I would, from the evidence collected, would have to admit that that is true, on the face of it," Goldwater acknowledged. "I wouldn't want to say that it is categorically true, because we investigated very few unions in the three years of our investigation. And during that time, where we found corruption, as you suggest, was amongst the old line craft unions, and we didn't find, well, I'd have to, I just can't think quickly of finding any extent of it in the industrial type union."

This lame and halting admission conveniently omitted any reference to the manner in which Barry Goldwater and his Republican colleagues had failed to get some damaging goods on Walter Reuther in the UAW-Kohler fiasco.

With facts and truth on one side and politics on the other, Barry Goldwater will choose politics every time. Nothing showed this more clearly than his performance in Savannah, Georgia, on October 2, 1960 during the Nixon-Kennedy campaign. There he proclaimed:

"The evidence is just too plain for us to assume anything other than the Kennedys protected Reuther for the political backing they are now getting in this campaign."

Goldwater, of course, did not specify what that "plain" evidence was.

CHAPTER XI

The Build-up Begins

In 1958, Barry Goldwater, up for re-election, had his own hand-made menace. The pursuit of Walter Reuther, which he had inspired, had fallen flat in Washington, but this made no difference to Goldwater. Reuther was, for him, the ideal foreign menace with which to scare the britches off the conservative electorate back in Arizona, and Goldwater based his campaign for re-election, not upon waging political war with his official opponent, Ernest McFarland, but upon furious battle with the man who wasn't there — Walter Reuther.

It is always better to run against Walter Reuther in absentia, a fact that Barry Goldwater had been brought painfully to recognize in the final debacle of the McClellan hearings. In Arizona, Goldwater didn't have to worry. There was no witness stand that Reuther could pre-empt for a forum.

The year itself was to be one of almost unmitigated disaster for Republicans. Senator John Bricker, the arch-conservative from Ohio and author of the Bricker Amendment that would have whittled away the President's power in foreign affairs (a radical innovation that Goldwater, incidentally, had supported), had gone back home to run for re-election on a platform that put heavy stress on the right-to-work issue. The Republican leader in the Senate, William Knowland, had torn the California Republican Party apart to get the gubernatorial nomination, hopefully expecting to build a Presidential image for 1960 and hopefully, in his ultra-conservatism, campaigning also on the right-to-work issue. Both Bricker and Knowland were defeated in upsets that left the Republican right-guard stunned and shaken.

But, in Arizona, Barry Goldwater, running this time without any assistance from Ike's coattails, carved out an impressive victory. His was the outstanding Republican success in the nation, with the possible exception of Nelson A.

Rockefeller's surprise election as Governor of New York; and this triumph against the strongly running Democratic tide was to build his national stature.

Goldwater began running a year-and-a-half in advance of the election, and he ran hard. From the very start, his entire campaign was pitched on the theme of the so-called union "menace." The initial barrage was fired as early as March 28, 1957 when Republican leaders, meeting in Tucson, heard State Chairman Richard Kleindienst call for the re-election of Goldwater. Kleindienst coupled this call with an attack on Gov. McFarland, who had defeated Goldwater's old buddy, Howard Pyle, for accepting a $4,000 campaign contribution from Jimmy Hoffa's Teamsters Union.

At another meeting on September 29, 1957 Republican leaders heard an even stronger denunciation of labor from Stephen Shadegg, who had masterminded Goldwater's first campaign and was to direct his second. Shadegg cried that labor "bosses" were prepared to spend at least a million dollars to defeat Goldwater. He charged that a New York public relations firm, once retained by Reuther, had offered a Phoenix concern $250,000 to run a "smear" campaign against Goldwater. "They don't want anyone in the Senate as fearless and articulate as Barry Goldwater," Shadegg declared.

There can be no doubt that the union leadership wanted to defeat Barry Goldwater in 1958, but there has never been a shred of evidence to support Shadegg's fantastic charges of a $250,000 offer to one public relations firm and an overall campaign kitty of $1 million. After the campaign, McFarland reported expenditures of $125,951, but even so his spending had not kept pace with Goldwater's. For Goldwater reported he had spent $202,717.

Some of Goldwater's contributions were intriguing. Texas oil money showed up prominently again. Cecil B. DeMille, of Beverly Hills, Calif., the movie magnate, sent $1,000. Henry R. Luce, of New York, the emperor of the *Time-Life* complex, contributed $500. And up in Massachusetts a man named Robert Welch, who was soon to leap to national notoriety as head of the John Birch Society, industriously passed the hat around for Barry Goldwater. He was later to claim that he had raised and forwarded to Arizona some $2,000 for use in Goldwater's campaign.

In an article after the election, Richard L. Tobin, of the North American Newspaper Alliance, was to attribute Goldwater's success largely to the heavy financial backing that poured into Arizona. "Friends of Goldwater," he wrote, "have obtained information that he received fat checks from scores of business and industrial leaders in every part of the country . . . as one White House deputy said: 'It almost always pays off. You've simply got to have the money to pay for a big campaign, and in this TV era the money factor is more important than ever.'" Barry Goldwater had the money. As Tobin pointed out, John Bricker, in Ohio, did not.

The union opposition to Goldwater was handicapped by the relative weakness of labor's position in Arizona. The CIO convention in Miami in the spring of 1958 had called for Goldwater's defeat, but there was little on-the-scenes organization. COPE, the political action arm of the AFL-CIO, established a branch office in Tucson, and its advice and the aid of its skeleton staff of workers were available to McFarland. This presence of union personnel on the scene, weak and generally ineffective though it was, helped to lend reality to Goldwater's charges of an "invasion" by the forces of foreign labor.

The theme of his campaign, pitched a full year and a half in advance of the election, never wavered. Barry, the All-American boy, was locked in battle dire with a Goliath — the union dictatorship and union gangsterism that threatened the American Way. Vice President Nixon lent his prestige to this theme, proclaiming in a statement: "I predict the voters in Arizona will show their resentment of Walter Reuther's attempt to purge him from public life."

Goldwater was for good people everywhere, even for those in the unions. He planted himself solidly in the corner of the poor, downtrodden laboring man; he was the poor fellow's champion — and everybody else's champion — against the ruthless forces of callous union leadership.

"They tell you that Barry Goldwater fights labor," he proclaimed. "What they should tell you is that I have been fighting the racketeers and gangsters and power-mad bosses who virtually hold the power of life and death over individuals in the labor movement . . . .

"I have nothing but contempt for union bosses who have stolen the funds of their fellow workers and would now try to steal their freedom by controlling the government of the United States."

The Pulliam-owned newspapers, the powerful *Arizona Republic* and the *Phoenix Gazette,* whooped it up for Goldwater. They quoted him in headlines almost every day, and it did not matter whether his thought for the day was old or new. McFarland, with considerable justification, accused the press of running a campaign of "fear and smear" against him, and one of his workers declared disgustedly: "If Goldwater recited 'Mary Had a Little Lamb,' the Pulliam press would make it the banner story of the day."

Witnessing this performance, one of the nation's more astute political observers, Marquis Childs, wrote words that in 1964 seem to have been loaded with prophecy. Childs commented that "the extremism indulged in here can only promote a widening of the division between labor and management. A crusade to set one part of the country in violent hatred against another part is hardly a service to the nation."

Childs wrote those words even before Goldwater's campaign had truly peaked. Shadegg, with the heavy campaign bankroll behind him, had astutely organized a television blitz for the closing days of the campaign. He had signed up every television station in Arizona for three half-hour programs on the same prime time. This meant that, nowhere in the state, during those three half-hours, could television viewers see anything but Barry Goldwater.

The theme of the telecasts was the unvarying and unrelenting one on which Goldwater had pitched his entire campaign — the labor "menace." In the first telecast, Gentleman Barry was presented live in stark contrast to selected film clips showing scowling, angry, belligerent union witnesses at the McClellan hearings. The shots put heavy emphasis on at least one appeal to prejudice; they stressed the testimony of UAW Secretary Emil Mazey, who had accused the Catholic clergy of alleged favoritism in the Kohler strike. Handsome, smiling, reasonable Barry seemed, by contrast, like a knight in shining armor.

The statewide telecast of October 29 introduced Barry to his TV public in dramatic and striking fashion. The program opened with the TV cameras trained on a montage composed of the front pages of union newspapers. The cameras focused on the paper screen long enough for the viewers to identify the papers and their headline attacks on Goldwater; then, through the middle of the screen, bursting it and tearing it aside, leaped Barry Goldwater.

Newsprint still clinging to his shoulders, he pirouetted before his TV audience.

"Now," he said, "you might take a good look at me — see if you can find the horns and tail."

Their absence established, Goldwater teed off on the labor "menace." He lashed at COPE, the AFL-CIO's political action committee, as "the mastermind of hate." He denounced Hoffa as the potential transportation czar of the nation, a "man who wants to have the absolute say-so over whether your children will get milk." He had, he said, gone to school "with a carpenter's son. The watchmaker's boy was my dear friend. The captain of our football team was the son of the blacksmith." Barry assured his viewers, still ,fascinated by his agile leap through the paper screen, that he had the deepest respect for such honest and honorable men of toil. That, he said, wasn't the issue in the campaign. The issue was "whether a United States Senator must be completely subservient to labor bosses and, because of political fear, accede to their every demand."

McFarland countered this blitz by putting heavy emphasis on his role as the father of reclamation projects in Arizona (an issue that, Shadegg later wrote, did not register at all with the voters, as private Goldwater surveys had shown) and by taking up television time reading letters from prominent Democrats endorsing his candidacy and wishing for his return to the Senate. It was a most uneven contest. And it was to be capped by a blunder that virtually assured Goldwater's re-election.

During the noon hour of Friday, October 31, some unidentified persons distributed a handbill in the shopping area of Phoenix. The anonymous leaflet, stuck under windshield wipers or deposited on the seats of open cars, featured a drawing of the late Soviet Premier Joseph Stalin. Stalin was smoking his pipe and winking. The caption read: "Why Not Vote for Goldwater?"

The smear enraged Goldwater headquarters, but a few moments' quiet reflection convinced the Goldwater brain trust that the cartoon was probably the best thing that had happened to them during the course of the campaign. The Goldwater people gathered up all the copies of the handbill they could get and distributed them to every television station and newspaper in Arizona. The resulting flood of publicity sparked a statewide reaction, and in the last days of the campaign Arizonans talked about virtually nothing except the outrageous smear attack on Barry.

McFarland's headquarters tried to counterattack, contending that the Goldwater camp had had the cartoon drawn and distributed itself. The rationalization seemed far-fetched, there was no evidence to support it, and it didn't convince very many voters. Investigations after the election showed, indeed, that two members of the International Association of Machinists had distributed the poster, but just who had originated and financed the idea never did become clear. The two distributors were later tried, convicted, and fined $1,000 each. Before this could happen, the voters of Arizona had made their decision. They sent Goldwater back to Washington by a vote of 164,593 to McFarland's 129,030, a margin of slightly better than 35,000.

This decisive verdict focused national attention on Goldwater, and no sooner had he returned to Washington for the opening of the new session of Congress in January, 1959, than a move was launched to make him again the chairman of the Republican Senatorial Campaign Committee. Goldwater's first two-year term had expired in 1957. Normally, a Senator would not be named so quickly for a repeat performance in this post of prestige. Obviously, somebody up there must have liked Goldwater. Just who remains a mystery. Only one thing seemed clear at the outset, and this was that Barry himself wasn't seeking the appointment.

The campaign to boost Goldwater into the campaign driver's seat stirred some misgivings in the more liberal Eastern wing of the Republican establishment. Senator Everett Saltonstall, of Massachusetts, chairman of the GOP Senatorial Conference Committee, was distinctly unhappy and made no secret of it. Liberal Senators like Jacob K. Javits, of New York, were dismayed at the prospect that they might be running for re-election on liberal platforms — while Goldwater cut across their campaigns by purveying his own brand of arch-conservatism. Senator John Sherman Cooper, of Kentucky, one of the Republican liberals haunted by this vision, protested that the selection of Goldwater would "give Democrats a chance to label the Republicans as anti-labor in 1960."

On the other hand, the more conservative of the GOP conservatives lined up behind Barry. Senator Everett Dirksen, of Illinois, whom the conservatives had recently made chairman of the party's policy committee, plumped for Goldwater. So did Styles Bridges, of New Hampshire, and Karl Mundt, Barry's associate on the McClellan committee in the days of contented squirrels and happy pheasants. Goldwater himself, though he had disclaimed originally that he was a candidate for the post, became an active battler for the job he didn't want as soon as it became clear he might not get it. He was surprised, he said in a statement to the press, to see Senator Saltonstall "yielding to the pressures of the labor bosses — the very ones whose intentions are to destroy the Republican Party and the very ones I defeated in the campaign."

Behind the scenes, potent forces were at work. Lyle C. Wilson, writing in the Washington *Daily News* of January 14, 1959, said that Goldwater had stayed in the race for the campaign chairmanship "because party contributors wanted it that way." Wilson added: "Their long-distance telephone calls of protest against bypassing Senator Goldwater were impressively numerous and angrily emphatic . . . Senate office telephone bells began to ring Friday morning. The morning papers had reported that Senator Saltonstall was counting Senator Goldwater out of the campaign committee chairmanship . . .

"Contributors from coast to coast rang in with protests against what they interpreted as an appeasement of labor leaders. They sharply reminded Republican Senators that organized labor's muscle and money long had been committed against the GOP. This was no sham battle between the right and left wings of the Republican Party as was the recent contest for the Senate party leadership. This dispute had bone and sinew."

This barrage by the party's fat cats was decisive. Just a week later all opposition collapsed, and Goldwater was renamed chairman of the Republican Senatorial Campaign Committee — a post that he was to use as a stepping-stone to his party's 1964 Presidential nomination.

Goldwater now became the national salesman of ultra-conservatism. As his party's Senatorial Campaign chairman, he was much in demand as a speaker at party fund-raising affairs, and he took advantage of the invitations that poured in, stumping the nation from one end to the other much as he had stumped Arizona in his political campaigns.

A typical Goldwater schedule found him taking off from Washington on Thursday. During the extended weekend, he would cram in speech after speech in a tightly planned schedule, and on Monday he would fly back to Washington to resume his Senatorial duties. Inevitably, his work in the Senate suffered. In 1960, for example, Goldwater missed 58 out of 192 roll call votes. Some of these were minor, but others weren't. He wasn't present to vote on the final passage of the civil rights bill, housing legislation, Latin-American aid, and other vital issues. In 1961, he missed 67 out of 207 roll calls and was absent in the final showdown on some issues on which, one would have thought, Goldwater would have liked to be registered, such as the Senate vote to give the President discretionary authority to grant economic aid to Communist-controlled countries and the Senate vote opposing the admission of Red China to the United Nations.

What Goldwater was doing, of course, was what came to him most naturally. He was not a legislator, as Taft had been. Not for him the meticulous attention to detail, the wearisome art of compromise and adjustment and revision in putting together a major piece of legislation. He was a salesman, and he was selling a creed, his own simplified, individualistic creed for rolling back the twentieth century.

He flitted about the country with furious energy; he sold, calm and reasonable though he was in personal appearance, with a kind of driven frenzy as if there might be no tomorrow. In the month of June, 1961, though the Senate was in session nineteen days, he made twenty-three speeches away from Washington. Invitations to speak poured in at the rate of twenty a day. Some 800 letters a day flooded his office. To handle the tidal wave of correspondence, a staff of thirteen labored in his suite of five offices in the Old Senate Office Building and in two more rooms in the basement.

This frenetic performance and the frenetic reaction it was inspiring were made possible by the jet age which placed even distant reaches of the nation only a couple of hours flying time from Washington. Curtis Steuart, a wealthy Washington businessman and long-time admirer of Goldwater, placed at his disposal an executive type DC-3 with its private crew. In addition, Goldwater had his own plane for shorter jaunts, and in his far-ranging safaris, he was greatly aided by his status as a reserve Air Force general. Goldwater commanded the 9999th Reserve Squadron, composed of Senators, Congressmen and their assistants — another prestige post since these were men who were in a position to vote more money for the Air Force, and so men whom the Air Force, not unnaturally, would like to please. The result was almost inevitable. As Drew Pearson wrote, "When Goldwater has a speaking engagement, he can usually get a plane for a 'training flight' to the town or general area where he is speaking."

The *Christian Science Monitor,* in a special dispatch from Evanston, Ill., on July 17, 1961, described how Barry swooped down out of the sky in the guise of a general in the Air Force Reserve, ducked into a taxicab and hastily changed from flying togs into dinner jacket to assume his role as purveyor of the political word to a waiting gathering. "He rolls out of a big Air Force jet at the local air base (O'Hare), still wearing his flying togs," the Monitor's correspondent on the scene reported. "He is a reserve Air Force Brigadier General, and he has been up in front with the pilot helping out at the controls in a one-hour-plus whiz-in to Chicago from Washington, D.C."

Just how frequently the dedicated apostle of the simplified life and fewer government services for everybody availed himself of the vast resources of the Air Force to whisk him places for the dissemination of his own special creed, the records don't disclose; but, as Al Capp pointed out in the Los Angeles *Mirror*, his continent-ranging jaunts, even if he had traveled by commercial airlines and regular highways, would have depended upon federal taxes and federal services (airports, radar, weather forecasting) for which commercial airlines did not begin to pay.

Behind the scenes, there were other indications that the lofty Goldwater crusade for the old-time virtues might have some seamy edges of its own. On January 3, 1961 Drew Pearson broke a story about Goldwater's lavish use of the Senate Campaign funds he handled. Pearson and his right-hand man, Jack Anderson, discovered that $4,000 a month was being paid from the party fund to the S. & K. Laboratories in Phoenix, manufacturers of a remedy for asthma known as Adreno-Mist.

Pearson noted with relish that "a good many Republican politicians were puffing and wheezing during the recent campaign as if they had asthma," but nevertheless he had the suspicion that $4,000 a month represented a pretty expensive cure for the party faithful so afflicted. He discovered after some investigation that S. & K. Laboratories really covered up the identity of Stephen Shadegg, Goldwater's two-time campaign manager and currently his ghost in the authorship of a widely syndicated newspaper column entitled, "How Do You Stand, Sir?"

Anderson telephoned Shadegg to inquire why the Senate Campaign committee was paying him $4,000 a month.

"I don't think that is any of your business," he quoted Shadegg as replying.

Anderson told Shadegg he would be perfectly happy with that quote and would use it. Shadegg reconsidered, finally explained: "I am a consultant to the Senatorial campaign committee."

Why, Anderson wanted to know, had the money been paid to S. & K. when really Shadegg was getting it? "The pay-

ments cover my work, expenses, travel — all sorts of things,"
Shadegg replied. He denied vigorously that he was getting
the $4,000 a month for his services as Goldwater's column-
writing ghost; but when Anderson persisted and wanted to
know why, in that case, the payment hadn't been made
directly to Shadegg, Shadegg "mumbled something about
'bookkeeping.'" It seemed intriguing to Anderson and Pearson that these camouflaged payments totaled some $40,000,
a price they considered somewhat excessive for the 300
pages of "campaign memos" Shadegg said he had produced.

Such disclosures had little perceptible effect on the Goldwater image. As Cabell Phillips, of *The New York Times,*
later noted:

"Few positions afford a politician more 'exposure' to other
politicians throughout the country than this. Day by day, by
letter, by telephone and in person, he is in touch with the
governors, state chairmen and other leaders of the party
who wield the influence that counts when it comes time to
write platforms and pick Presidential candidates. If he is a
good chairman, as Mr. Goldwater is generally conceded to
be, he builds 'a line of credit' with party leaders in the key
states on which he can draw when the need arises."

Barry Goldwater was indefatigable in building this "line of
credit," and when the showdown came in 1964, he drew
against it at his party's convention in San Francisco.

CHAPTER XII

Goldwater's Stands

Goldwater, who had accused the Eisenhower Administration of a "betrayal" of Republican principles in its first term, lashed out at it in its second for attempting to run a "dime store" New Deal. He was increasingly critical and increasingly outspoken as the Eisenhower era rolled downhill to 1960. The whole trend of the administration was too far to the left to suit him; and when Arthur S. Flemming, Ike's Secretary of Health, Education and Welfare, proposed a medical care program for the aged, Goldwater's ire boiled over.

"This," he proclaimed in May, 1960, "is but another act in the strange drama of an Administration which gives full support to a sound dollar, and a balanced budget, and less federal control, but which in actuality has suggested time and time again measures which mean more federal control, measures which result in less chance to balance our budget, and measures which attack the value of our dollar.

"We could well call these actions the 'dime store' New Deal. We have said for nearly thirty years that the welfare state, centralized government, and federal control are wrong. But in spite of that, we say a little of it is all right.

"We are against federal aid to schools, but we have suggested a little of it; we are against federal aid to depressed areas, but we have offered a plan for a little of it; we recognize that to increase the minimum wage would be inflationary and would result in unemployment, but we suggest a little increase; we have constantly held that the federal government should not provide socialized medicine, but now a spokesman offers a plan for a little of it . . ."

Goldwater was against it all. He was against so much that it seemed at times as if he was against everything. But there were two, or perhaps three, notable exceptions.

107

He could be counted on to favor more money for the military — and especially the Air Force. He was always for legislation that might help big business. And reclamation projects in Arizona somehow didn't represent the great "socialistic" evil that other types of projects did.

Significantly, the one action in which Goldwater takes most pride was his lonely stand against the Kennedy-Ervin Labor Reform Bill in 1959. The bill was designed to correct the evils exposed in the McClellan investigation, but Goldwater contended it was so weak it was a cover-up. The Senate passed the bill by a vote of 95 to 1, with Goldwater alone in opposition. Subsequently, the House of Representatives drafted and passed the much stronger Landrum-Griffin Act; and, though this measure wasn't strong enough either for Goldwater's taste, he considered it so much better that he worked for its passage in the Senate. Landrum-Griffin in the end was substituted for the Kennedy-Ervin bill with only two dissenting Senate votes — a complete reversal of the Senate's original position and a result that has led Goldwater at times to rate this as his one most important action in twelve years in the Senate.

The overall Goldwater performance in those years has been analyzed by *Congressional Quarterly* in a compilation that paints a picture of the man. During his first term, he supported the Bricker Amendment to curb the President's treaty-making powers. He voted for the Natural Gas Act, which would have allowed producers to raise rates without federal interference. He voted against the proposed federal Hells Canyon Dam project — but for the Upper Colorado reclamation project, vital to Arizona. In 1957 and again in 1959, he voted to table moves to alter the Senate rules, an important maneuver in the civil rights fight; and in 1957, he voted for the Civil Rights Act — but only after siding with the Southern bloc to limit its application to voting cases and to guarantee jury trials in all cases of criminal contempt, hampering provisions that tended to negate its effect in the South.

On the domestic front, Goldwater stood solidly against virtually every sort of federal activity. In addition to his opposition to such proposals as medicare and federal aid to education, he voted in 1959 against increasing federal grants for sewage plant construction from $50 million to $80 million. In 1960, he opposed authorizing $251 million in federal aid to depressed areas, and in 1961, he fought $394 million for area redevelopment grants and loans. He was against authorizing $655 million to train unemployed workers; against federal participation in urban mass transit projects; against passage of the Youth Employment Act — and for a measure to kill the Youth Conservation Corps.

Goldwater's votes on tax measures fell into a pattern that was doubly significant, as significant for what he favored as for what he was against. He opposed a measure raising the personal income tax exemption from $600 to $700, and it was perhaps significant that this same measure would have deleted provisions granting dividend exclusions and tax credit. He favored a $6 billion tax cut in 1958 and looked favorably upon reducing the taxes on small corporations, raising them on large. But he opposed the repeal of the 4 per cent tax credit on dividend income; fought any reduction of the depletion allowances for oil and gas interests; denounced the proposal to impose a 20 percent withholding tax on interest and dividends; favored the reduction of top-level income taxes from 87 to 60 per cent; and declared himself again against any reduction of oil and gas depletion allowances, this time on a bill that would have imposed such reductions on a taxpayer only when his gross income exceeded $1 million a year. Does one discern in such votes a consistent pattern of opposition to the interests of the great mass of the taxpayers, and in accord with the special desires of the big money men who had so handsomely bankrolled Goldwater's campaigns for election?

There were those who definitely did come to such conclusions. Goldwater's votes in 1961-62 were rated an absolute zero by Americans for Democratic Action, the AFL-CIO and the National Farmers Union. Labor statisticians said, indeed, that Goldwater had never voted "right" in labor's view on any issue of importance in his twelve years in the Senate; he was, they said, the only Senator or Representative, holding office for such a length of time, who rated that distinction. On the other hand, the ultra-conservative Americans for Constitutional Action, those voting index is the bible of reference for the John Birch Society, rated Goldwater 100 percent.

The voting record is like a skeleton exposing what a man stands for and what he is against, but the true nature of that standing becomes vivid only when one listens to his actual words and phrasing on specific issues. In the Congressional session of 1960, Senator Kennedy, soon to become his party's nominee for the Presidency, advocated an increase in the minimum wage from $1 to $1.25 an hour.

From the outrage of the conservatives, one might have expected some cataclysm to rend the heavens and destroy the world. A debate in the House-Senate conference committee wrangling over the provisions of the Kennedy bill furnished an insight into the motivations of some of the principal actors.

Kennedy began by reproaching Senator Dirksen for worrying about extending federal power in interstate commerce if the bill should pass and the minimum wage should be raised a whole quarter an hour.

"I have never heard you raise your voice against federal policing of labor strikes," Kennedy told Dirksen. "But now, when we are trying to make employers raise the wages of underpaid workers, you suddenly get quite excited about interstate commerce."

Goldwater broke in, arguing that "most of our big retail establishments are already paying a decent wage."

Retail clerks in major stores, he said, were averaging $1.75 an hour.

"Well, if that's the average in the stores you speak about, why are you and these same stores and big business lobbyists against a minimum wage of only $1.25 an hour?" asked Rep. John Dent (D., Pa.), a former rubber worker.

"Now, wait a minute," said Goldwater. "I didn't say all retail employers are paying $1.75 to their help. Many can't afford it. They pay less."

"You're damn right they pay less, and you and the other opponents of this legislation would like to keep it that way," Dent snapped. "In fact, there are more than 10 million workers in this country now getting $1 or less an hour, though living costs are increasing all the time."

In argument on the floor, Goldwater led the opposition to the Kennedy minimum-wage hike. In an impassioned four-and-a-half hour speech, he argued that the bill could result in unemployment, inflation, socialization of the economy and damage to the Constitution.

"This is a great bureaucratic plum," Goldwater intoned, picturing the quarter-an-hour pay boost as the creator of a veritable chamber of horrors. "I can see them now. Thousands of bureaucrats down there licking their chops, ready to crack business over the head . . . I don't think there is an economic problem in America that the free enterprise system cannot solve."

This is an oft-proclaimed, bedrock faith of Goldwater's. He is a man who speaks emotion, whose forte is reaction rather than study. This leads at times to a self-exposed simplicity and naiveté of the mental processes, revealing how little he has made contact with the problems of the twentieth century. One such exposure came on *CBS Reports* on March 8, 1962 at the hands of Eric Sevareid.

Referring to Goldwater's clamor that big federal government is becoming a despotism, crushing the freedom of the people, Sevareid asked a simple question: "Who in this country is unfree?"

"Well, as of today, it'd be difficult to point out a person and say, 'He is unfree,'" Goldwater conceded.

However, he said, thirty percent of our farmers who came under the Agricultural Act had lost the freedom to decide what they would plant and how much; compulsory union membership, he considered, made the workers "unfree"; and, of course, the federal government was taking in taxes about a third of what a man earned, denying him the right to spend that much of his own income.

Sevareid wanted to know if there weren't "some deep reasons" for changes on the American scene. Goldwater acknowledged that there were, that "a little bit of it seems pretty good," and that, in fact, you could make out "a pretty good case for socialism," except that "I don't believe in it. I think it's the ruination of governments and people."

Well, said Sevareid gently, let's take the welfare program. Goldwater apparently felt that relief should be a private not a public concern:

"What I would prefer . . . is the private individual taking care of his brother. Now, if this doesn't come about, and it doesn't in every case, then the church, fraternal organizations, and so forth, companies, corporations should assume their part of the responsibility, and again, if they don't, then you go to the local government. If they don't, State government, and, if they don't, you cannot deny a person help. We're not going to stand by and see people die or suffer, and if it has to get to the federal level, there is nothing we can do about it."

Sevareid questioned Goldwater's stated thesis that federal relief and welfare programs had been created, not out of need but "out of the minds of planners." Did Goldwater think that people in slums should be "content with their lot?"

No, they shouldn't be content, Goldwater said, "but their neighbors, somebody who lived with them in the same town and possibly knew them," should take on "this chore of relieving their distress." The innocence of the Goldwater mind in thinking naturally of "town" when Sevareid was thinking just as naturally of "slums" was thrown into high relief in this sequence:

SEVAREID: Senator, what about places like Harlem or South Chicago where millions of people hardly know one another? Many of them can hardly speak the same language. Who's going to take care of them?

GOLDWATER: Well, the — how are they faring under the federal government? They're still there. They're still living in squalor . . . .

SEVAREID: But you would remove government relief?

GOLDWATER: No, I'd like to try it. I'd like to see us encourage the areas that I've discussed to do this . . . . now, if they won't do it, then we can't — it's senseless to talk about it, but I'd like to see us try.

He was then led to talk about the progressive income tax. In response to a Sevareid question, Goldwater said flatly (he was later to smudge this clear-cut stand as the Presidency loomed nearer): "Yes, I'm against that." He explained: "I think it's wrong to have one man pay one rate and another man pay another rate. It's a tax on a man's ambition . . . ."

SEVAREID: But if you do not have the graduated income tax and everybody paid the same percentage, it would be primarily a tax on the poor and the middle class, wouldn't it?

GOLDWATER: No, not necessarily. If a man makes $5,000 a year, and he's not exempt from anything, his share would be the same share as a man making $50,000 or $100,000. I think that fairness appeals to Americans, and this would not be a burden on the poor, or the middle-class.

That kind of reasoning might make Barry Goldwater H. L. Hunt's favorite economist, but it is to be doubted if the average American, who would inevitably have to bear a far heavier load, would be enchanted with this Goldwater criterion of "fairness."

The absurdities to which Goldwater could give solemn expression through the technique of simplification probably were never better illustrated than in some of the columns he began producing in January, 1960. The columns, ghosted by Shadegg, appeared originally in the *Los Angeles Times* and ultimately achieved a wide syndication throughout the nation. The early columns invariably began by asking the question: "How do you stand, sir?" This was followed by a proposition so absurdly oversimplified that the reader was left with only one spot of ground on which to stand.

Some examples illustrate the point. These, taken at random, are typical of the Goldwater technique and tone. "How do you stand, sir? — for voluntarism or compulsion?" "How do you stand, sir? — for maximum opportunity or for a stereotyped, carbon-copy society?" "How do you stand, sir? — for citizen responsibility or governmental dictation?" "How do you stand, sir? — for liberty or for slavery?"

The body of the columns usually did full justice to the intellectual quality of the opening proposition. For example, in the column of February 6, 1960, Goldwater asked: "How do you stand, sir? — for equality of opportunity or equality of achievement?" He then wrote that "the radical liberals" appeal only to greed and envy and "believe in equality of achievement." Making clear the meaning of this dogmatic revelation, Goldwater wrote: "The radical liberal is saying that in his broad democracy one hapless alcoholic drifter is equal to one Jonas Salk; one ne'er-do-well is equal to a Steinmetz or an Edison; one crooked gambler equal to one great theologian."

From the mass of Goldwater columns, a dominant impression emerges. The suave and sometimes charmingly self-deprecatory exterior concealed a mind militarily oriented, a mind suspicious of civilian conspiracies, a mind that sought a hard world of rigid order and the regimentation of all resources for the final trial by force with the heathen antagonist. All of this was advocated, paradoxically, under the frantically waved banner of freedom and liberty, with profound obeisance to the goal of peace.

The tone of fanaticism and demagogy was unmistakable in the columns he produced for four years before, on the podium of the Cow Palace, in his acceptance speech, he placed the official seal on extremism and wrapped it in the folds of the flag. No one who had taken the trouble to read Goldwater should have been surprised. For example, in a column on March 20, 1960, calling for an all-out effort against the pagan ideology of communism, Goldwater wrote:

"I pray for the voice of an American leader who will challenge the people of this nation to foget their happy luxuries, the leisure of their five-day weeks, the bitter and destructive conflict now raging between segments of our society and turn their strength to the task of demonstrating that freedom is superior to slavery on any battlefield the Russian masters may choose."

He wrote frequently that American foreign policy had been "traveling the wrong road," that negotiation was fruitless, that co-existence was a fraud and a delusion, and that the only solution lay in "achieving a victory through the defeat of communism." He was to magnify this, in his book, *Why Not Victory?*, into a call for "total victory" — all by methods not defined, at price carefully unspecified.

The rigidity, the militaristic cast of the Goldwater mind has led him at times into the defense and justification of military dictatorships. Attacks in America on the growing power of the military-industrial complex, attacks stemming in large part from President Eisenhower's compelling emphasis on the problem in his farewell address, have infuriated Goldwater. Those who worry about the possible take-over of American institutions by the military, he wrote, "do not understand the military mind. Nor can they bring themselves to study it." Military men, Goldwater explained in his column of October 9, 1962, must operate on principles that have been proven and tested, not on any newfangled, untried liberal ideas.

"I suggest the military man of today is overwhelmingly conservative . . . ," he wrote. "Because of this the chance of communism taking over when armies are in charge of bankrupt, fallen, unstable governments is at best remote."

In most cases in which military men had overthrown established governments, he added, "They have been forced to act . . . when the orderly processes of government failed. In other words, in most places where the military has acted, it has acted because extreme circumstances prevailed." Turning to Cuba, Goldwater has looked back with fond regret on the Batista regime, and he has intimated the proper solution to the Cuban problem might be for us to install a dictator on the unhappy island and keep him there.

"A friendly dictator might be the answer . . . ," he told Sigma Delta Chi in a Washington speech in the spring of 1963. "We would be better off in Cuba today with Batista . . . . If we had realized what he [Castro] was originally we could have given enough aid to Batista to crush him."

The man who favors such militaristic solutions, who boggles not at dictatorship so long as it is a dictatorship of the right, invariably votes for more abundant and more costly military hardware. Any suggested military cutback or military curb brings Goldwater out fighting. The abandonment of the Skybolt project shocked him more than it did the British, who had hoped to keep their bomber fleet alive with the air-to-ground missile; the cancellation of Dyna Soar outraged him; and he exploded in several columns on the idiocy of the civilian heads of the Defense Department in refusing to pour billions of dollars into full-scale development of the Air Force's pet 2,000-mile-an-hour RS-70 because the bomber had been outmoded by the age of missiles.

The presumption of civilians in thinking they should decide such matters incensed the military partisan in Goldwater. In an interview with United Press International in March, 1963, he declared the Kennedy administration was duplicating the mistakes of Hitler and the Kaiser by listening to civilian rather than to military advice. "I say fear the civilian — they're taking over," he cried shortly afterward in a speech to the Military Order of the World Wars in San Antonio, Texas.

Proposals to slash domestic spending, on the other hand, were hailed by Goldwater. In this same March, 1963, he devoted an entire column to enthusiastic reception of a proposal to slash President Kennedy's domestic programs. The President had sent to Congress what he described as a bone-hard $98.8 billion budget, and he had challenged Congress to cut it. Almost instantly, Senator A. Willis Robertson (D., Va.) suggested $6 billion could be slashed. Robertson would have cut $1.2 billion from aid to education; $495 million from the Rural Electrification Administration; $350 million from area redevelopment; $1.8 billion from foreign aid; $489 million from the National Science Foundation; $1 billion from the National Institute of Health. He also urged a five percent across-the-board reduction in government personnel and a $1.2 billion trim in military spending. Though Goldwater almost certainly wouldn't have approved any cutback of military spending, he was ecstatic about the drastic proposals to cut back, if not totally cripple, a broad spectrum of education, science, health and welfare programs.

The insensitivity to the lot of ordinary human beings patent in these ideological contrasts sometimes became so obvious that portions of the press, ordinarily conservative, were moved to swat at Goldwater. One such incident occurred in mid-February, 1961, when Goldwater swooped into Louisville, Kentucky, on one of his missions as the salesman of ultra-conservatism. The country had been in a deep recession in the last months of the Eisenhower era, and one of Kennedy's first moves had been to initiate a spending program to spur the economy. Goldwater declared he saw no need for this. The nation's economy, he said, was in good shape; there were just a few spotty areas. Cracking like

McCarthy, he added: "Labor Secretary (Arthur) Goldberg
. . . has pushed the panic button — a button painted red."

Goldwater's performance made the Louisville *Times* see
a different kind of red. It ran an editorial entitled "Goldwater and Marie Antoinette." If Louis XVI's queen had ever
advised that the half-starved people of Paris should eat
cake, it would have been, said the *Times,* "no more cruel
(or fatuous, depending upon the intent) than some of the
things Senator Barry Goldwater said here in Louisville Saturday." The *Times* accused Goldwater of "a blithe refusal to
face facts." He had had, said the *Times,* "the effrontery" to
say that things were good "in a city which had just been
classified as a substantial area of unemployment, in a state
in which one person out of nine is receiving federally
donated food." Goldwater's sneer at Secretary Goldberg
also incensed the *Times.* "The unsubtle innuendo is clear:
that those who dare assert the economy has slowed down and
who have compassion enough and energy enough to want
to help the unemployed are in some unspecified way Communistic, are 'painted red,'" it wrote. "We might remind
Senator Goldwater that had not another group of men in
the early '30's acted with energy and compassion this country
might now conceivably be Communist."

The Goldwater attitudes which had not endeared him to
the *Times* and the people of Louisville created at the moment
nothing like the storm he was soon to arouse with his proposal to sell the Tennessee Valley Authority, the great public
power and development project on which most of the prosperity of the area is based. Goldwater's backers in this
campaign year of 1964 will tell you solemnly that their
candidate never made such a proposal, but he did. And not
once but several times.

One of the first mentions of his sell-TVA fetish came in
a speech on June 19, 1961 before the National Association
of Plumbing Contractors in Detroit.

". . . For example, I know many of you are from the South
and you probably are acquainted with the Tennessee Valley
Authority," he said. "I think this type of government-in-busi-
ness thing should be turned over to free enterprise, even if
they could only get one dollar for it. We would get more
back in taxes out of TVA in a matter of five years than
we've gotten out of it since the thing started. And that
would apply to all federal power projects across this country
wherever private power can operate."

This initial statement didn't receive very prominent press

coverage or really set tempers boiling in the Tennessee Valley. But all calmness vanished in a puff of angry smoke when Goldwater restated his views in a long interview with Stewart Alsop, of *The Saturday Evening Post*, in September, 1963. Alsop questioned Goldwater on a number of points and reproduced the vital part of the interview in question-and-answer form this way:

REPORTER: You have been quoted as saying that you'll oppose the progressive income tax, that everyone should pay the same rate.

GOLDWATER: Yes. Yes, I still believe that.

REPORTER: But do you really think it's fair that a man with five million a year should pay the same rate as a man with five thousand?

GOLDWATER: Yes. Yes, I do.

(Goldwater explains that the poor man would benefit from the rich man's investments, while in his mind's ear the reporter hears liberal orators make mincemeat of candidate Goldwater as "the rich man's candidate" in 1964.)

GOLDWATER: (Volunteering) You know, I think we ought to sell TVA.

REPORTER (scribbling busily): You really do?

GOLDWATER: Yes. Yes, I do.

(Ooops, thinks the reporter, there goes the whole Tennessee Valley.)

The storm broke almost instantaneously, and the kindest thing said about Goldwater was that he had exhibited colossal ignorance. His imputation that TVA was a dead cat hung around the taxpayers' necks simply wasn't true. As the Chattanooga *Times* pointed out on November 4, 1963, TVA sold its power to the public at rates far below those of privately operated utilities — and, at the same time, it actually paid out more in taxes than many of them did. In 1961, the *Times* wrote, TVA paid $51,432,000 into the federal treasury and $17,355,000 in state and local taxes. A survey of twelve neighboring privately owned utilities showed that they paid from 4.8 percent to 11.4 percent of their revenues in state and local taxes; TVA paid out 7.3 percent, a rate exceeding that of five of the private companies. All this, said the *Times*, had been accomplished by TVA despite the fact that its consumers were getting power at $3.63 per 200 kilowatt hours, a rate approached only in the Pacific Northwest, where, incidentally, there was also public power.

These were the indisputable facts which Goldwater had ignored, and it was obvious that the residents of the Tennessee Valley were thoroughly cognizant of their good fortune — and enraged at Goldwater. The mail that descended upon his office ran two to one against him, his own aides said, and the opposition was even heavier than that in the TVA area. "I have contributed to your campaign and helped to organize a Goldwater club here . . . but since you have . . . come out . . . for sale of the TVA, I am taking off my Goldwater stickers," one disenchanted supporter wrote in a letter whose reproachful tone was milder than that of many.

What especially incensed the Tennessee Valley was that Goldwater, at the same time he wanted to dismember TVA, if only for one dollar, was struggling his hardest to get through Congress a bill that would create a super-TVA on the Colorado in his own state of Arizona. TVA had cost $2.5 billion in 30 years — and had repaid $417 million of it. But Goldwater's pet project, which envisioned higher and larger dams than TVA had, five of them on the Colorado and one on the Gila, was estimated to cost some $3.1 billion in the next 15 to 20 years. It would generate enormous quantities of power, control floods, store water for irrigation — all those things that, to Goldwater, were anathema because they represented the dangerously "socialistic" hand of the federal government. Yet Goldwater saw no evil, heard no evil, spoke no evil here. He seemed genuinely unable to recognize the elementary fact that he had trapped himself in a glaring inconsistency.

The attitude came through clearly in his disastrous January, 1964 appearance on *Meet the Press* immediately after he had announced his Presidential candidacy. He still, he said, wanted to dispose of TVA. Marianne Means reminded him that he had sponsored, for central Arizona, "one of the largest federal water projects that was ever proposed before Congress. Don't you see any moral and ethical inconsistency here?"

"Oh, why, there's none at all," Goldwater replied. "There's no comparison between TVA and the Central Arizona project. It's not a public works project, to begin with; it will pay back at least 85 per cent of the money invested in it by the federal government — and we all live under the reclamation law."

Other laws apparently do not apply to all of us; the reclamation law is unique — and no threat to the American Way.

CHAPTER XIII

Gateway to the Pinnacle

The year 1960 unlocked the future for Barry Goldwater. It was a year that began with a column and a book; it was a year marked by Republican defeat — and so a year that left Goldwater, as one of his aides astutely forecast at the time, his party's "receiver" in bankruptcy.

The book that had so much to do with furbishing his ultra-conservative image was published in March, 1960. It was called *The Conscience of a Conservative;* it was written with the assistance of Brent Bozell, an editor of the right-wing *National Review* and one-time ghost of Joe McCarthy; and it sold hundreds of thousands of copies in hard-cover edition and paperback.

A compendium of absolutes, *The Conscience of a Conservative* saw public problems in all-white, all-black terms, with no shadings even for the most complex issues; and it called for simplistic, all-out, either-or solutions. Central to its message were the irreconcilable paradoxes of Goldwater-ism: on the one hand, the idea that federal government should be decentralized, with vital power returned to the localities and the states, a conception that, to use a Goldwater phrase, must have had Alexander Hamilton doing "snap rolls up in heaven"; on the other hand, in diametrical conflict, the passionately proclaimed belief that we are engaged in a holy war against communism, that all muscle must be marshalled for that war — and that it must be won totally, completely, even at the cost of a world-incinerating nuclear holocaust.

Goldwater saw the federal government as "a Leviathan, a vast national authority out of touch with the people, and out of their control." He would dismantle this. His ideal was to elect a President "who is pledged to enforce the Constitution and restore the Republic. Who will proclaim in a

119

campaign speech: 'I have little interest in streamlining government or in making it more efficient, for I mean to reduce its size. I do not undertake to promote welfare, for I propose to extend freedom. My aim is not to pass laws, but to repeal them. It is not to inaugurate new programs, but to cancel old ones that do violence to the Constitution, or that have failed in their purpose, or that impose on the people an unwarranted financial burden. I will not attempt to discover whether legislation is "needed" before I have first determined whether it is constitutionally permissible. And if I should later be attacked for neglecting my constituents' "interests," I shall reply that I was informed their main interest is liberty and that in that cause I am doing the very best I can.' "

No paragraph Goldwater has ever written more clearly expresses the absolute negativism of his approach to government and issues in the infinitely complex twentieth century. Government in this concept would never govern; it would not attempt to regulate or to mediate; it would not attempt to help or improve; it would not attempt to contend with the great social crises of the day — it would simply turn all back to the town meeting and the states. Here was the genesis of Goldwater's vote against the 1964 Civil Rights Act; and in *The Conscience of a Conservative,* years before that testing-time of conscience, he had clearly stated the ground on which he stood.

He wrote that "the federal Constitution does *not* require the States to retain racially mixed schools. Despite the recent holding of the Supreme Court, I am firmly convinced — not only that integrated schools are not required — but that the Constitution does not permit any interference whatsoever by the federal government in the field of education."

This conviction led him inevitably into a denunciation of the Supreme Court. The court, in his view, was usurping powers never granted to it by the Constitution. In passages that made him the white knight of the white supremacists of the South, he declared that he was "not impressed by the claim that the Supreme Court's decision on school integration is the law of the land . . . . The Constitution is what its authors intended it to be and said it was — not what the Supreme Court says it is."

In another passage, Goldwater declaimed: "The Congress and the States, equally with the Supreme Court, are obliged to interpret and comply with the Constitution according to their own lights. I therefore support all efforts by the States, excluding violence of course, to preserve their rightful powers over education."

This proposed dismembering of the federal establishment on the home front was coupled with a call for aggression on the international scene. Goldwater saw the Communist world as a monolith of evil, united, dedicated, determined to conquer every square inch of the globe. In the light of the soon-to-be-revealed, deep and bitter schism between Russia and China, in view of the accumulating evidence of cautious assertions of their independence by the Communist regimes of Eastern Europe, Goldwater's fanatic view of a cohesive menace, untroubled by internal discords and dissensions that might work to our advantage, seems decidedly unrealistic. But it is a view to which he tenaciously holds, a view that leads him to refer disparagingly to "peace" and look with equanimity on the possibility of war.

The intemperance of Goldwaterism, which alarms our closest European allies and leaves them shocked and stunned at the possibility that he might ever become President, rings out clearly in passages such as this:

"If an enemy power is bent on conquering you, and proposes to turn all of his resources to that end, he is at war with you: and you — unless you contemplate surrender — are at war with him. Moreover — unless you contemplate treason — your objective, like his, will be victory. Not 'peace,' but victory. Now, while traitors (and perhaps cowards) have at times occupied key positions in our government, it is clear that our national leadership over the past fourteen years has favored neither surrender nor treason. It is equally clear, however, that our leaders have not made *victory* the goal of American policy . . . .

". . . We want a peace in which freedom and justice will prevail, and that — given the nature of Communism — is a peace in which Soviet power will no longer be in a position to threaten us and the rest of the world. A tolerable peace, in other words, must *follow* victory over communism . . . .

"We do not, of course, want to achieve victory by force of arms. If possible, overt hostilities should always be avoided; especially is this so when a shooting war may cause the death of many millions of people, including our own. But we cannot, for that reason, make the avoidance of a shooting war our chief objective . . . ."

Take all the sugar-coating off the pill, and this, clearly, is a policy that might well lead to war. Goldwaterism means, as Goldwater himself acknowledges, taking all the awesome risks involved in the most aggressive brinkmanship. The extent to which Goldwater would be prepared to go in this life-and-death poker game was clearly spelled out in an interview with Chesly Manly for a Chicago *Daily Tribune* profile. Here is Manly's rendering of Goldwater quotes:

"American policy must be geared to the offensive . . . We should encourage the captive people to revolt against their Communist rulers . . .

"We must ourselves be prepared to undertake military operations against vulnerable communist regimes. Assume we have developed nuclear weapons that can be used in land warfare, and that we have equipped our European divisions accordingly. Assume also a major uprising in Eastern Europe such as occurred in Budapest in 1956.

"In such a situation we ought to present the Kremlin with an ultimatum forbidding Soviet intervention, and be prepared, if the ultimatum is rejected, to move a highly mobile task force, equipped with appropriate nuclear weapons, to the scene of revolt.

"Our objective would be to confront the Soviet Union with superior forces in the immediate vicinity of the uprisings and to compel a Soviet withdrawal.

"An actual clash between American and Soviet armies would be unlikely; the mere threat of American action, coupled with the Kremlin's knowledge that the fighting would occur amid a hostile population and could easily spread to other areas, would probably result in Soviet acceptance of the ultimatum.

"The Kremlin also would be put on notice that the resort to long-range bombers and missiles would prompt automatic retaliation in kind. We would invite the Communist leaders to choose between total destruction of the Soviet Union and acceptance of a local defeat.

"I believe such action in Hungary in 1956 would have stopped communism dead in its tracks."

World War I, the tragic and senseless war that triggered a century of conflict and turmoil, resulted from just such infantile and optimistic miscalculations that the opponent would yield to the ultimatum and would never fight.

Even Goldwater himself, in his more candid moments, has acknowledged that the percentages, as he sees them, favor war over peace. In his 1961 conversations with Irwin Ross, he conceded: "Some day, I am convinced, there will either be a war or we'll be subjugated without war." He made it clear that he wasn't talking about any piddling, brushfire conflict — but about a major nuclear holocaust. "I think that a general war is probable," he told Ross. "I don't see how it can be avoided — perhaps five, ten years from now." Wasn't he appalled, Ross asked, at the prospect of the utter devastation a nuclear war would bring? Goldwater answered philosophically: "Every generation has feared the increased devastation of war." It seemed to escape him, perhaps purposely, that in the twentieth century we are not talking about "increased devastation," but the utter destruction of the world and all its people — the extinction of mankind.

Those who might have missed the Goldwater message in *The Conscience of a Conservative* should have been left in no doubt if they read their daily newspapers. For on March 16, 1960, in a widely reported speech in the Senate, Goldwater put his program into the official record. He advocated:

Withdrawal of diplomatic recognition from Soviet Russia.

Continued nuclear testing by the U.S. and the rejection of any permanent ban.

Elimination of foreign aid — and the substitution of American private enterprise.

Abolition of the exchange program on the grounds it was "simply another operation in Communist political warfare."

Less reliance on the United Nations (soon Goldwater would be toying with the idea we should get out of the U.N. altogether).

"This is hard counsel," Goldwater told the Senate. "But it is hard, not for what it says, but for saying it openly. It is hard counsel because it frankly acknowledges that war may be the price of freedom, and thus intrudes on our national complacency . . . ."

Goldwater's speech provoked a rift in his own party. Senator Sherman Cooper (R., Ky.) said bluntly: "The worst thing that could happen right now would be to withdraw American recognition of Russia and refuse to negotiate." The only possible way to relieve world tensions, he said, was by negotiation.

In this same month of March, 1960, in which *The Conscience of the Conservative* made its bow, in which Goldwater spelled out his program in the Senate, the tom-toms of the Far Right began to beat in furious cadence, drumming up for Goldwater the image of big things to come. In New Bedford, Massachusetts, the extremely conservative *Standard Times* produced a glowing series — and secured for it national syndication — suggesting Goldwater as "a possible candidate for either the Presidency or the Vice-Presidency."

Asked about this, Goldwater disclaimed any connection with the drumbeating and fell back on the charming modesty that is so disarming.

"Naturally, I'm flattered by such offers," he said, "but I think that's as far as they'll go."

He was wrong, as he may have suspected at the time. On March 26 he went to Columbia, South Carolina, to deliver the keynote speech to the Republican State Convention. He was in rare form and gave what was described as "a rousing address." He flayed the New Dealish Eisenhower budgets, expressed his contempt for "modern Republicanism" — and applauded the Southerners for their "steadfast devotion" to principle in the civil rights battle. He had hardly finished when Roger Milliken, of Spartanburg, one of the nation's more prominent textile magnates, took the floor and urged the convention to instruct its thirteen delegates to vote for Goldwater for the Presidential nomination. The suggestion was greeted with a rebel yell. And the Goldwater boomlet was spawned.

Born in fanaticism, it was never to know moderation. Goldwater, making a test run, trying out his artillery for the future, became more shrill, more irresponsible. With the same blithe disregard of facts with which he had inspired the phony Reuther probe, he continued to belabor the Kennedys with charges of a Democratic whitewash; and, as Jack Kennedy's nomination became assured, his vituperation passed the bounds of what many would consider common decency. On June 10, 1960, the Indianapolis *Star* quoted Goldwater as saying this:

"I sincerely fear for my country if Jack Kennedy should be elected President. The fellow has absolutely no guts or principles. Money and gall are all the Kennedys have . . . ."

This was the kind of language that made the passion juices flow in the glands of the dedicated. On July 6, 1960, just a couple of weeks prior to the gathering of the clans for the Republican National Convention in Chicago, the Chicago *Daily News* reported the formation of an organization known as Americans for Goldwater. It established headquarters in an abandoned bake shop in the Loop, and its staff was a mixture of old pros and young, eager volunteers.

In the next four years, there was to be much journalistic yakking and confusion about the extent of Barry Goldwater's involvement with the Radical Right. To many it seemed incredible that personable, reasonable-seeming Barry could himself belong to the lunatic fringe, and the comforting and widely accepted theory developed that, while he couldn't afford to disclaim such support, he wasn't really a part of the movement. He was just a decent guy who was the captive, or half-captive, of a flock of extremist followers.

Such an interpretation seemed logical to many Americans, for we are essentially an innocent people and it seems inconceivable to us that a Respectable may be just as radical in his own way as the loudest ranter. Yet a better understanding of recent history and of the tides of ultra-conservatism in America should have dispelled such comfortable rationalizations. Fascism itself, as the history of the movement in Italy and Germany had amply demonstrated, results precisely from the welding of the power and talents of the Respectable and the Radical. Behind Mussolini were the Italian industrialists; behind Hitler, the Krupps and the military. For Respectables, desirous of protecting and retaining — and perhaps extending — the power and privileges conferred by wealth, the Radical is indispensable; he is the demagogue who lathers mass emotions and makes possible the attainment of the desired end. The Respectable, in his delusion, expects always, of course, to be able to control his Radical front man and comes only too late to the realization he has been devoured by the helper he financed and supported. Still the delusion persists.

In America, though the objective seems never to have been the establishment of a fascist dictatorship, it has been and definitely remains the complete takeover of the government by the same combination of forces — and by use of the same propagandistic, rabble-rousing, even strong-arm methods — that, in Europe, resulted in the Fascist and Nazi tyrannies. So it becomes necessary to analyze with great thoroughness the powers behind the launching of the Goldwater Presidential candidacy in 1960.

The original spokesmen for Americans for Goldwater were Frank C. Brophy, a retired Arizona banker, and Clarence Manion, former dean of the Notre Dame law school, a member of the Birch Society's governing board and the proprietor of the Manion Forum, an ultra-right propaganda program heard weekly over some 200 radio stations across the nation. Also prominent among the original organizers of the Goldwater boom were Walter Harnischfeger, Milwaukee industrialist; Hubbard Russell, wealthy California rancher; Paul

H. Talbert, wealthy California real estate man; and Robert
B. Dresser, a Providence, R.I., attorney.

A complex of right-wing organizations, many of them on
the far-out fringe, also joined up for the battle. They included: We, the People!, For America, the Wake-Up
America Committee, the Anti-Fluoridation League, the
Defenders of the American Constitution, Pro-America, and
the National Education Program, of Searcy, Arkansas, an
idea factory for the Radical Right with an expressed sym-
pathy for the John Birch Society.

Individuals in the supporting cast of sponsors were equally
noteworthy for their strong right-wing fixations. They included Herbert V. Kohler, president of the Kohler Company,
whose cause Goldwater had championed in his futile effort
to "get" Reuther; Merwin K. Hart, one of the nation's
veteran anti-Semites; Mayor J. Bracken Lee, of Salt Lake
City, an avowed hard rightist; Mrs. Ruth Murray of Oshkosh,
Wisconsin, national co-ordinator of Vigilent Women for the
Original Bricker Amendment; and Generals G. E. Strate-
meyer, Albert C. Wedemeyer and Bonner Fellers. Wedemeyer served for a time on the advisory board of *American
Opinion,* the official organ of the Birch Society.

At the center of this amalgamation of right-wing forces
were men like Clarence Manion and Hubbard Russell who
had been active for years in For America. Manion, indeed, in
addition to his leadership role in the Birch Society, had been
co-chairman of For America, serving with Maj. Gen. Robert
E. Wood, retired, former president of Sears, Roebuck & Co.
and long a supporter of right-wing causes. The program of
For America, in the light of its sponsorship of the Goldwater
candidacy, is highly intriguing.

Its manifesto, headlined in bold type, "The Disaster We
Face," trumpeted: "International leadership has captured
both parties. Internationalist policies undermine American
Independence, threaten us with bankruptcy, involve us in
FOREIGN WARS and are destroying our liberty." For
America advocated repeal of the income tax, getting the
U.S. out of the U.N., ending "foreign bribery by giveaways,"
elimination of all government competition with private enterprise (as in TVA), support of Congressional investigations
"into Communist-Socialist activities," an end of "compulsory
unionism" and the eradication of "socialism in America."

The advocates of these doctrines had been searching for
years for a personable leader to make them politically viable.
Hubbard Russell, proprietor of the Rancho Cuyama in Mari-

copa, California, had described this search in a confidential memorandum he circulated among the forces of the right following a cross-continent safari he made in June of 1954. He wrote that he had cast his first Presidential vote for William Howard Taft and "will always regret that I was cheated by the 'King Makers' out of voting for his son Robert in 1952." He was, he said, doing "all I can in re-establishing Constitutional Government as it was until wrecked by the 'New Dealers' and 'Me-Tooers.'"

During his tour in search of a leader, he met and talked with a wide cross-section of prominent public figures who, he said, shared his concern and wanted to do everything they could to "save America." In Chicago, Hubbard conferred with Col. Robert McCormick, publisher of the arch-conservative and isolationist *Chicago Tribune;* in New York, with Gen. Wedemeyer and former President Herbert Hoover; in Washington, with Eisenhower's unpopular Secretary of Agriculture, Ezra Taft Benson, with Vice President Nixon, with Fulton Lewis Jr., with David Lawrence and Nobel Robinson of *U.S. News & World Report*, with Senators Knowland, Goldwater, Bricker, Pat McCarran of Nevada, and Harry F. Byrd of Virginia. In summarizing the impressions he brought away from all these high-level contacts, Hubbard wrote:

"Whenever one of us would say, 'the country is ready for a fighting leader,' these officials and Congressmen and Senators seemed to agree . . . It appears that a great many people, such as most of those interviewed, are still looking for leadership, and they are pretty badly disgusted and disappointed . . . To a man, they are worried about spending, high taxes, unbalanced budgets and foreign relations. Many expressed worry because so many Truman-Acheson holdovers are still formulating a lot of policy. Some said the wrong men were still advising and no apparent way to stop it . . ."

This theme that the Eisenhower administration had been infected with an insidious left-wing virus by holdovers from the Truman era was to become a favorite of Goldwater's; he was to use it repeatedly in future years to explain what he considered the dangerous leftward slant of the second Eisenhower administration. In the circumstances, it probably is not surprising that he and Hubbard Russell evidently discovered their kinship as early as 1954. Russell, in his memorandum, described Goldwater as "an outstanding, courageous young Senator," and six years later he had so high an opinion of Goldwater that he became one of the prime movers in promoting the Goldwater candidacy.

Such were the forces that tried to get a Goldwater boom off the ground in Chicago in 1960. Their aim was to get Goldwater on the ticket, if not for the Presidency, then for the Vice Presidency. Manion claimed there had been a "tremendous grass roots swell" for Goldwater "and his devotion to conservative, constitutional government." Using the favorite argument of die-hard conservatives, he claimed that "the great majority of Americans" wanted Goldwater's brand of government, "but there hasn't been a conservative nominated they could vote for in more than 20 years."

There was not to be in Chicago in 1960. Nixon made his midnight deal with Rockefeller to liberalize in faint degree some of the planks of the Republican platform, and the eastern "King Makers," as Russell called them, threw their support behind a Nixon-Lodge ticket. Goldwater and his followers were incensed. "Obviously angered," according to *The New York Times,* Goldwater denounced the platform deal as "a surrender to Rockefeller" and "a Republican Munich." For a time, he threatened an open floor fight against the platform; but, after counting noses, he abandoned the idea.

So Goldwater made his famous television appearance before the convention, projecting the image of a handsome, attractive man, a good loser, a good team player. The result, as one observer noted, was that he emerged from the convention "as the undisputed and highly articulate spokesman of the GOP Old Guard."

Such impressions sometimes endure — and sometimes fade. Goldwater's backers were determined that his should not be one to fade. The zeal and determination that fired his ranks — and that were to make the events of 1964 possible — were most imperfectly appreciated at the time. Only Laurence C. Eklund, of the Milwaukee *Journal,* seems to have been perceptive enough to sniff the breeze of the future. In an article on July 26, 1960, he wrote that the Goldwater legions were already preparing for a Nixon defeat, if Goldwater didn't get second-place on the ticket — and that they were looking ahead with plans to pick up the pieces in 1964.

Reginald Mitchell, public relations man for Americans for Goldwater, took Eklund bluntly:

"If and when the Republican Party goes down the drain in November as the result of the failure to put Goldwater on the ticket in this convention, it will go into national receivership, and Goldwater will be the logical man to take over as receiver."

Much of the 1963 speculation that Goldwater didn't really want to run, that he would prefer to remain Senator from Arizona, might have been avoided if more attention had been paid to that frank avowal of purpose; if the eastern Establishment, so long in control of the party, had correctly evaluated it and the determination of the forces of the Radical Right. As it was, all of these tell-tale signs were ignored until it was too late — ignored, too, in spite of a dead giveaway by Goldwater himself.

Not that Goldwater didn't campaign for the Nixon-Lodge ticket. He did. He rampaged up and down through the Southern States, the Southwest and the Midwest, wearing out his lungs and his larynx. The election of Kennedy, he told a Florida audience, "would put the final nail in the coffin that would seal forever our constitutional government." He denounced medicare, aid to education, Walter Reuther, labor bosses in general, the hiking of the minimum wage. He wanted to "eliminate" Castro and intimated the U.S. should use "air power, marines, the whole works." He denounced the U.N., telling the Executives Club of Chicago: "Most Americans reading their newspapers this morning wonder whether it might be a good idea to move that capitol some place else, so we don't have to put up with that murderer's row — those rogues walking around the streets of this country."

In the midst of it all, Barry dropped a pretty plain hint that he might have his eyes focused already on 1964. On October 8, 1960, almost a month before the election that was to seal Nixon's defeat and make Kennedy President, United Press International moved a dispatch out of Phoenix that began: "Senator Barry Goldwater has announced his availability as a 1964 Republican Presidential candidate if Vice President Nixon should fail to win next month." The story said Goldwater emphasized, "I'm for Dick Nixon," but he added that, should Nixon be beaten, "I will not hesitate to submit in 1964 for the Presidential nomination . . . ."

No words could have been plainer. And hardly had Nixon succumbed before Goldwater rushed to stake out his claim for the next time around. In an interview in Phoenix on November 9, 1960, he laid the blame for the defeat squarely on Nixon's shoulders.

"We who are conservatives," he said, "will stoutly maintain that 1960 was a repeat performance of 1944 and 1948 when we offered the voters insufficient choice with a me-too candidate."

Nixon, he said, had lost the election by gambling for votes in the industrial North at the expense of opportunity in the South. "I told them that at the convention," Goldwater said. Implicit in this was the suggestion that the Republicans should have wooed the white supremacist vote in the South.

Implicit, too, was the suggestion that things might be different the next time — when Barry Goldwater would be running the show.

CHAPTER XIV

The Birch Stain

Dwight David Eisenhower was "the most completely opportunistic and unprincipled politician America has ever raised to high office . . . ." He was "insincere, vindictive and hypocritical." Harry Truman was "too dumb" to realize he was being used by the Communists, but Eisenhower had no such excuse. He was "the *only* man, Russian or American, or of any other nation, who was ever allowed to have his picture taken with Stalin (just the two of them together) at the tomb of Lenin . . ." And all this could mean only one thing — that Dwight David Eisenhower, hero general and hero President, the most beloved American of his generation, had been "a dedicated, conscious agent of the Communist conspiracy."

In those capsuled quotes, one has an open window into the deluded mind of the man who wrote them — Robert Henry Winborne Welch, Jr., the founder of the John Birch Society, the organization that Barry Goldwater has never disavowed.

No issue can be more important in the campaign of 1964. Here is the capstone of principle. On the one side are the free and open processes of American democracy, with its reliance on freedom of thought and debate and decision; on the other, the fascistic tactics of Radical Right extremism, with its reliance on smear and intimidation, strong-arm methods and violence. Barry Goldwater, the Phoenix Country Club McCarthyite, never has been willing to repudiate the extremists whose minds in so many matters are in tune with his own; but, in San Francisco, accepting his party's nomination, he went the one fateful step farther — he flatly endorsed extremism, flatly condemned "moderation in the pursuit of justice." The false face of personal charm and reasonableness disappeared, and the mind and commitment of the fanatic stood exposed.

The fullest exposure of this world of folly and delusion has been afforded by the activities of Welch and his Birch Society; for that society, with its infinite cross-ties to other Radical Right prophets and organizations, serves to bind together and to coalesce the yeasty ferment of the Far Right.

The Welch view of the world we live in has been explicitly stated in two books, his privately published *The Politician* and *The Blue Book* of the John Birch Society. In *The Politician* (the title referred to Eisenhower), Welch besmirched the characters of many prominent Americans. Welch wrote that he was convinced Dr. Milton Eisenhower, Ike's brother, was probably "Dwight Eisenhower's superior and boss within the Communist Party." General Marshall, author of the Marshall Plan that saved Western Europe from communism, was to Welch a "conscious, deliberate, dedicated agent of the Soviet conspiracy. . . ." Welch incredibly believed that John Foster Dulles, with whom anti-communism was a religion, was "a Communist agent"; that Franklin Roosevelt was guilty "of plain unadulterated treason"; that Nelson Rockefeller was planning "to make the United States a part of a one-world Socialist movement"; that Chief Justice Earl Warren should be impeached because "he has taken the lead in . . . converting this republic into a democracy" and because democracy is "a weapon of demagoguery and a perpetual fraud."

It says much about the fateful coalition of Respectable and Radical in modern American society that, when Welch first expressed these views, the Respectables did not react in a respectable way; they did not shun Welch as if he had the plague. Instead, they listened to him, accepted him, and in the end lent him the power of their pocketbooks and the prestige of their names. The result was the creation of the John Birch Society, named after an OSS captain who was killed by the Communists in China and whom Welch had decided to turn into a martyr. The society was founded after Welch had talked for two straight days to a select audience of highly placed Respectables. The meeting was held in Indianapolis, Indiana, on December 8 and 9, 1958, and in attendance were millionaires who headed oil, textile and other businesses. One of them (and possibly two) had been former presidents of the National Association of Manufacturers.

Welch had given these Respectables *The Politician* to read, and they told him bluntly it wouldn't do. After all, they were not quite so deluded as to believe Dwight Eisenhower had ever been a Communist. On the other hand, it does not seem to have occurred to them that the man who could seriously promulgate such a fantasy was irresponsible and hardly qualified to become the leader of a principled cause; or, if this did occur to them, they plainly did not care. They, in effect, told Welch to come up with something else, and so Welch did. The candy manufacturer from Belmont, Mass., himself for seven years a director of NAM, discoursed for two days on his view of the world and his plans for the John Birch Society, a monologue that was recorded and became the basis of *The Blue Book*.

The Birch Society was to be a completely monolithic organization, with Welch its self-appointed Fuehrer. It was to have an advisory, governing board, but Welch's word was to be absolute. The society would be guided by three major principles: an attitude of eternal suspicion and secret investigation of everybody (for everybody can be suspected of being either a Communist or a sympathizer, a Comsymp); the doctrine of reversal, a weird exercise in logic that contends everything is the opposite of what it seems; and the avowed intent to use every "mean and dirty" tactic necessary to achieve the ultimate end — the world of Robert Welch.

It was, clearly, a world that banished reason, that repudiated the processes of democracy, that promoted chaos. Supremely ludicrous and chaotic was Welch's proudly proclaimed "principle of reversal." This held that the Communists are so wily they mean the exact reverse of what they say. If they profess peace, they mean war. They have devised this tactic of "reversal" in Welch's view to delude the good and the innocent, so that the good and the innocent will go out and work for the very causes the Communists secretly want. Looked at through a one-sided prism (if the Communists preach peace, they mean war), the "principle of reversal" is ideally tailored for Welch's demagogic ends; but, in all logic, it can lead only to a chamber of horrors. When the Communists trumpet war, do they really mean peace? When Robert Welch attacks communism, is he secretly — but let's not utter *that* thought.

The attitude of eternal suspicion and eternal spying, each man upon his neighbor, advocated by Welch as fundamental doctrine, would create inevitably a world in which no man would be free. Welch instructs his Birchers to gather all possible information on "Comsymps," on "the background connections and activities of all the leading liberals." Students should keep records of the words and conduct of their teachers; textbooks should be scanned — and exorcised if they make the slightest favorable mention of the U.N. This is a world, like the insane world of Hitler, that would clamp smothering repressions on the mind; that would inspire children to spy and report on their parents; that would make fact, knowledge, reason the pawns of fanatic ideology.

For Welch, the end justifies any and every means. He advocates the hiding of Birchite activities behind innocent-seeming fronts (just as the Communists do), and he makes no secret of the fact that violence is perfectly appropriate in the holy cause — "in defense of liberty," as Goldwater phrased it. The theme of violence is unmistakable in Welch's pronouncements. In his *Blue Book*, he talks constantly about "cancers," especially "the cancer" of collectivism. Welch argues that, "even though it is of considerable growth, [it] can be cut out. And despite the bad scars and the loss of some muscles, this young, strong, great nation, restored to vigor, courage, ambition and self-confidence, can still go ahead to fulfill its great destiny. . . . but we do have to achieve the sufficiently drastic surgery." As for tactics, consider this Welch pronouncement: "These tactics are mean and dirty, but the Communists are meaner and dirtier, and too slippery for you to put your fingers on them . . . no matter how much they look like prosperous members of the local Rotary Club."

This background has to be understood if one is to appreciate the persistent evasiveness of Barry Goldwater's reaction to the very grave issues posed by the Birch Society. His favorite tactic is to point an accusing finger at what he regards as the "radical liberal" left in the Democratic Party, with special emphasis on one of his favorite whipping-boys, Americans for Democratic Action. It is a response that obdurately ignores two vital points: what the Birch Society admittedly stands for, and the fact that there is no possible comparison with what the ADA stands for. ADA has never advocated a national spy-vigilante system, has never promoted violence in any form, but has devoted itself to promulgating its liberal views in the free exchange, the give-and-take, of the democratic system.

Bearing these distinctions in mind, let's take a look at the Goldwater footwork on the Birch issue. Goldwater had known Welch for a long time and considered him a good friend. About 1956, he says, while Welch was visiting his brother in Arizona, the future leader of the Birchers stopped by Goldwater's home and left a copy of *The Politician*. Goldwater acknowledges that this probably made him one of the first persons in the nation to see and read the book. He didn't like what he read, he says, and he returned the volume to Welch with the advice that, if he couldn't prove everything he had written, he had better destroy the work.

"I told him in strong language that if his book were discovered and he couldn't prove anything in it, he would be destroyed," Goldwater told Irwin Ross in 1961.

But what about the Birch Society itself? Ross wanted to know.

Goldwater said he deplored Welch's "dictatorial" role, but: "On the other hand, I know a number of good people in both parties who belong to the group. I take the position there's nothing wrong in what they're trying to do, but their leader has made some absurd statements. I'm not satisfied that these people have done any great damage. I'll grant you that in some parts of the country they've got some bits to answer for — I know they've called Milton Young a Communist — but the people of my state haven't done it."

Ross commented drily: "North Dakota, which Young serves as a Republican Senator, is obviously a far country."

Goldwater persisted in his rationalizations and justifications of Birch Society extremism. On November 19, 1961 he appeared on *Meet the Press*, and Lawrence Spivak grilled him about his stand on extremist groups like the Birchers and the Minutemen:

GOLDWATER: I would say that the Minutemen would comprise a danger because they violate a charge of the Constitution [by carrying arms] . . . . The Birch Society, from what I can hear of them, constitute no danger. I am far more concerned, frankly, with the extremists of the left than I am with the extremists of the right.

SPIVAK: I know. You think that the John Birch Society is not led by an extremist?

GOLDWATER: I would say if Bob Welch is a leader today that he would be an extremist, yes.

SPIVAK: Well, he is the leader.

GOLDWATER: But he does not occupy a position in government, as do many people of the extreme left.

Spivak tried to find out whether Goldwater would want

the Birchers to play "a leading role" in his political movement. Goldwater wouldn't answer directly. He hedged that the only Birchers he knew were those in Phoenix and that they "have been interested in anti-communism, they have never backed a candidate, they have never taken a position on an issue, and I certainly cannot consider these people dangerous."

Spivak pointed out that, in a speech just the previous day in Atlanta, Goldwater had said: "The real extremists are the people to the left, the Socialists in the Kennedy Administration." Just who were some of these Socialists in the Kennedy Administration, Spivak asked. Goldwater mentioned Arthur Schlesinger, Jr., the Harvard professor and historian who had become a White House adviser, and Ted Sorenson, the principal draftsman of Kennedy speeches. These and other members of the ADA in the administration constituted the socialist menace he had in mind, he said. "Now they are in. The Minutemen, the members of the Birch Society are not in government. They are on the outside. I cannot understand this threat —"

Goldwater's attitude became most clear during these same months of 1961 in which he was taking violent evasive action on the Birch issue. Where, on the one hand, he was seeing no harm in the Birchers, he was on the other proclaiming the positive good that he felt was being done by a lot of other super-patriotic groups. One of his most explicit commendations was in a column on March 14, 1961 praising a rally staged in Phoenix by Dr. Fred C. Schwarz, the Australian evangelist who had been selling a Birchite brand of anti-communism to the American people.

Dr. Schwarz's vehicle was the Christian Anti-Communism Crusade, with headquarters in Long Beach, California. The evangelist himself sometimes exhibits deep resentment at being classed with the Radical Right. He authors, he says, no political program, as does Welch; he is merely a "teacher," expounding on the face and evil of communism. But, listen to this typical Schwarz exhortation:

"Christians, to arms! The enemy is at the gate. Buckle on the armor of the Christian and go forth to battle.

"With education, evangelism and dedication let us smite the Communist foe and if necessary give up our lives in this noble Cause!

". . . We cry, 'We shall not yield! Lift high the blood-stained banner of the Cross and on to Victory!'

". . . Co-existence is impossible . . . Communism is total

evil . . . its methods are evil and its ends are evil . . . We must hurl this thing back into the pit from whence it came!"

Throughout 1961, backed by eminent business and military sponsorship, Schwarz ranged widely across the country, conducting so-called "schools" to indoctrinate the uninitiated. In the wake of Schwarz's passionate performances, converts went out with fanatical, missionary zeal to spread the new gospel, holding meetings in living rooms, American Legion halls, school assemblies and club rooms. Observing it all, one woman school teacher in Winnetka, Illinois, remarked to Cabell Phillips of *The New York Times* that her family had lived in Nazi Germany, and she asked: "Have you ever thought of the parallel between John Birch and Horst Wessel? I have, and it frightens me when I see this anti-Communist feeling getting out of hand."

Barry Goldwater had no such ideas. Regarding Schwarz's performance in Phoenix, he wrote:

"I have been greatly encouraged recently by reports from my Arizona office of the success of the Greater Phoenix Anti-Communism School. Thousands of my fellow Arizonians heard such crusaders for freedom as W. Cleon Skousen, Herbert Philbrick, Dr. Frederick Schwarz and others outline and catalogue the true nature of communism.

"My correspondents tell me this was the most successful anti-communism school in regards to members attending and money raised which has ever been held in the United States. My encouragement stems from an entirely different facet of the reports coming to me.

"The men and women who attended this school were community leaders; they were not fanatics; they were, in fact, sober, industrious, thoughtful citizens who have helped us shape the culture and the prosperity of the Southwest."

The ties that were being forged between Goldwater and the Radical Right became more evident in March, 1962, when the basement of Goldwater's Department Store in Phoenix became the rallying ground for another off-shoot of the proliferating fanatical organizations. This one was called The Anti-Communist Movement of Arizona (TACOMA), a wing of the Christian Crusade headed by the Rev. Billy James Hargis, of Tulsa, Oklahoma, an evangelist with ties to Clarence Manion, the Birchers and virtually every other major group active in the Radical Right field. Hargis is one of the true batting champions in the "against" league. In one speech, he condemned communism, liberalism, the National Council of Churches, federal aid to education, Jack

Parr, federal medical care for the aged, Ed Sullivan, the
Kennedy-Khrushchev meeting, Eleanor Roosevelt, disarma-
ment, Steve Allen and the Freedom Riders. He's also against
integration, which he has called "mongrelization."

Considering the man and his doctrine, no one should have
been much surprised by the performance in Goldwater's
basement. According to the *Arizona Journal,* which devoted
a full-page spread, with pictures, to the event, the main
feature of the first TACOMA session was a taped speech
by R. Carter Pittman, Georgia's anti-Red, anti-Negro propa-
gandist. Pittman charged that American Negroes were
"worse than useless" in World War II and that "the only
difference between the Congolese and the American Negro
is the Congolese eat more white people than those in
America."

These views so infuriated one of the audience, Renz
Jennings, an Arizona Supreme Court Justice, that he stormed
out of the meeting as soon as Pittman's appeal to race
hatred had ended. W. A. Robinson, a retired school principal who had invited the judge to attend, agreed with him
that the speech was "junk; just junk." But TACOMA continued to meet in Goldwater's basement, scheduling other
speakers of the Radical Right, including some connected
with the Birch Society.

These ties and associations, the bent of Goldwater's own
mind as revealed in his speeches, his column, his books,
caused relatively little alarm. Goldwater was a wealthy businessman, a flawless dresser; he had an attractive smile, an
engaging personality; he was a he-man who appealed to men
and women. Definitely, he was a Respectable; and it
seemed inconceivable to many Americans that, under this
conservative and highly acceptable exterior, there dwelt a
mind, fanatical in its views and orientation, that made him
blood brother to Welch and to Schwarz and to Hargis.
The theory developed (and endured until the acceptance
speech in the Cow Palace) that Goldwater himself was not
deeply committed to the Radical Right, that he was merely
using a political ploy because there were votes to be had by
it.

Irwin Ross, for example, asked Goldwater if his situation was not analogous to that of Henry Wallace in the
1948 campaign when much of Wallace's strength came from
communistic sources he could not afford to repudiate. Goldwater, Ross reported, simply smiled and did not deny the
validity of the comparison. At times, Goldwater himself

seemed to suggest that perhaps he wasn't really serious; that he was just indulging in a political tactic to bedevil the opposition. In mid-August, 1961, he told the Washington *Star* that he believed liberals were becoming confused and frustrated because conservatives were hanging the socialist label on them.

"It is becoming harder and harder for American liberals to explain away the fact that the programs they advocate are moving us closer to the kind of central government and control encompassed by socialism and that the socializing of societies plays into the hands of the communists." Goldwater added: "No American likes to be called a Socialist or to think that something he espouses is kindred to communism."

Whether Goldwater was merely playing political games or expressing honest belief, the effect was much the same. He was lending his impressive personality, his voice, his stature to the Radical Right; he was promoting Radical Right doggerel; he was wrapping himself and his Radical Right brethren in the folds of the flag, proclaiming that only theirs was the true patriotism and that anyone who disagreed was a Comsymp or traitor to his country.

Typical was his performance before the ultra-right *Human Events* conference in Washington in mid-July, 1963. *Human Events* is a newsletter financed by ultra-right millionaires and foundations. Goldwater had written for it in the past; and in his speech before the conference, he attempted, by indirection at least, to impugn the loyalty and motives of President Kennedy. Kennedy, he said, appeared "determined to co-exist with international communism wherever it thrives — even in the western hemisphere." He accused all liberals of suffering "a craven fear," of taking the nation "too far to the left;" and he charged that Gus Hall, the Communist leader, had urged his followers to seek the defeat of Republican candidates in 1964. Having by these innuendos spattered every Democrat in sight and linked them one and all to the dark devices of Moscow, Goldwater then protested that he was not suggesting, heavens, no, that the Democrats or the New Frontiersmen were Communists or that the Communists had captured control of the Democratic Party. So he attempted to preserve the lofty image of a Respectable.

Senator J. William Fulbright, the intellectual and independent Democrat from Arkansas, almost alone in the Senate seems to have appreciated Goldwaterism and its alliance with the Radical Right for the menace that it represented. Alone, he had spoken out in a memorandum denouncing the Radical

Right seminars that were peddling a fascistic kind of super-patriotism and fanaticism to the American people. He repeatedly had challenged Goldwater to spell out in specific terms what he meant by his pulse-raising cries for "total victory." How could it be achieved, Fulbright had demanded, except through total nuclear war that would leave the whole world in ashes? Goldwater had never met the challenge of specifics; he had simply continued to proclaim, as if the mere proclamation were an end in itself, that "total victory" should be our goal.

Now, with Goldwater's *Human Events* performance as a springboard, Fulbright rose in the Senate an August 2, 1963, and in a speech dripping with irony he "thanked" Goldwater for the "remarkable" speeches he had been making. It was a positive "relief," said Fulbright, to hear Goldwater's calls for "bold" policies abroad and "fundamentals" at home. It made everything so delightfully simple. Of course, he said, the Senator had never made it clear to anyone quite what it was all about, but the Democrats would not be so rude as to ask him.

"I, for one, am prepared to wait," said Fulbright. "It is rumored that the Senator may be prevailed upon to seek higher office. Should that be the case he will undoubtedly spell out a dynamic program of national action under some stirring title like 'The Fundamentals of Illiberalism' or 'Let's Get the Government out of the Business of Government.'"

Referring to Goldwater's charge that the Democrats were somehow Red-tainted because they had decided to co-exist, Fulbright pointed out that the meaning of the word was simply "to exist together at the same time."

"The Senator, as we all know," he said, "is unalterably opposed to such an arrangement between the Communist countries and the free world. It would seem to follow that the Senator considers it essential for one side or the other — presumably the Communist side — to stop existing at once. The problem, of course — which the Senator has not yet seen fit to comment on — is precisely how the Communists can be persuaded to terminate their existence."

In the world of nuclear bombs and intercontinental ballistic missiles, Fulbright pointed out, "the only alternative to 'co-existence' is mutual destruction. This perhaps is the key to the foreign policy favored by the Senator from Arizona — a 'bold,' 'courageous' and 'determined' policy of 'co-annihilation.'"

CHAPTER XV

Filling the Vacuum

The election of 1960 was hardly history, Kennedy had been in office as President for only a few months, when automobiles throughout the nation began to blossom out with bumper stickers reading, "Goldwater in '64." The stickers were appearing in profusion in a number of states by early May, 1961.

This visual evidence of the kind of dedication that was to kick off a four-year struggle for control of the GOP was completely misread by the liberal eastern Establishment. Since bumper signs are usually displayed only in the heat of a campaign, the premature Goldwater stickers were dismissed as the evidence of the aberration of a few crackpots. The eastern Establishment, with the short-sightedness that was to be its undoing, simply could not take the jet-age cowboy and his fanatic followers seriously, not even though another event occurred in this same May of 1961 that projected the Goldwater image in new dimensions.

This was the election in Texas to fill the U.S. Senatorial seat left vacant by Lyndon Johnson's ascension to the Vice Presidency. The Democratic machine in Texas had appointed as Johnson's successor a strong conservative, William A. Blakley. It was a move that split the Democratic Party, whose liberal wing detested Blakley, and offered the Republicans a gilt-edged opportunity.

The Republican candidate was John G. Tower, a chunky, round-faced, 35-year-old college professor and an arch-conservative of the Goldwater stamp. Sensing a chance to break the Democratic grip on Texas, national leaders of the GOP offered to campaign for Tower. Nixon, needing a forum to keep his image alive, was especially eager to lend a helping hand. Tower at first accepted his offer; but afterward, thinking it over, he changed his mind and asked Nixon to stay away. This rebuff resulted from Tower's feeling that Nixon was too "middle-of-the-road," a little liberal, a little conservative. Tower wanted none of that. He was hard right all the way.

The result was that only strong conservatives like Goldwater, Senator Thruston B. Morton of Kentucky (who was to be permanent chairman of the 1964 convention), and Rep. Walter H. Judd, of Minnesota, were welcomed in Texas as medicine men for the Tower campaign. Goldwater, indisputably, was the star of this visiting road show. He stormed all over the vast state, flying from one rally to another, and everywhere he went he drew huge crowds. Other speakers would get bursts of applause for their attacks on the Democratic opposition; but when Goldwater purveyed his fire-eating brand of ultra-conservatism, he brought down the house. He was unquestionably the star the voters had come to see and hear; and when Tower was elected, the first Republican to go to the U.S. Senate from Texas in ninety years, Goldwater was given major credit for the victory. It was the first time he had demonstrated his vote-getting appeal outside of Arizona. It was a triumph that said plainly Barry Goldwater was no purely local phenomenon; he was a power to be reckoned with on the national scene.

The enthusiasm of the ultras for the personable champion they had at last discovered after years of search knew no bounds. It went to such extremes that William F. Buckley's *National Review*, the ideological bible of the far right, ran a full-page advertisement on July 17, 1962 under the heading: "BE THE FIRST IN YOUR PRECINCT TO OWN A BARRY GOLDWATER SWEATSHIRT."

The ad explained:

"You'll delight in watching liberals recoil in terror when they see you in your BARRY GOLDWATER SWEATSHIRT. You'll find your BGSS imbues you with renewed courage to suffer the slings and arrows of the extremist lunatic fringe on the ultra left.

"The Barry Goldwater Sweatshirt [made in gentlemen's sweat shops] displays a nearly life-sized head of Barry Goldwater, with his name below to identify him to uninitiated liberals."

The sweatshirts, selling for $3.95 each, were obtainable from the Conservative Book Store, 228 Massachusetts Avenue, Indianapolis, Indiana.

While wearers of the sweatshirts presumably were striking

terror in liberal hearts, the fantastic upsurge of Goldwaterism throughout the nation was beginning to make some members of the GOP have second thoughts. They couldn't understand the basis of Goldwater's popularity, and they sometimes tended to discount it because it seemed to cut squarely across the prevailing political tides of the time. But undeniably, and in some mysterious, inexplicable way, the man was creating a stir.

Many efforts have been made to analyze the fundamental roots of Goldwaterism. Though Goldwater himself scoffs at the idea that he possesses political sex appeal, there can be no question that he has in marked degree that indefinable "star" quality, that personal *charisma* which no scientist has yet been able to dissect and reduce to a precise equation. The impact of this political asset on special groups is little short of devastating. Goldwater's handsome appearance, his engaging manner, his charm, his male ruggedness send women's gatherings into shrieks of ecstasy. The same qualities, plus his rousing appeal to patriotism and his advocacy of final solutions, have brought youthful legions flocking from college campuses to his banner.

This last phenomenon is one that has baffled many observers. Historically, youth in America has tended to be liberal in its orientation. A common American pattern, one so common that it has formed the basis of many gags, is for the socialist of twenty to become the conservative of middle age. The natural tendency, then, is to think that the college campuses would be the least fertile grounds in the nation for the flourishing of Goldwater's arch-conservatism. Goldwater himself refused to accept this view. He spoke at college campuses at every opportunity, and before anyone quite realized what was happening, he began to pack academic halls and draw audiences in the thousands. How, many asked themselves, could this possibly be?

As Goldwater himself sometimes points out, youth tends to rebel against the creeds of its elders, and in America for years, the older generation, nurtured on the reforms of Franklin Roosevelt, had been predominantly liberal. Rebellion, then, might explain part of the Goldwater phenomenon, but only part. Almost certainly another factor, and perhaps a larger factor, was to be found in strong, underlying, psychological impulses. Youth, by the very exuberance of its nature, dislikes drawn battles and protracted solutions; it seeks instinctively the quick and final answer. Tensions and frustrations unlike those any previous American generation has had to face have been the lot of this one — and the end, if the appraisal is honest, is not yet even remotely in sight. And so, in this perspective, it is perhaps not so astonishing as at first it might appear that arch-conservative Barry Goldwater, waving the flag and preaching "total victory" over the infidel, has become the Pied Piper of a segment of young America.

His success, the specter of the future implicit in it, were enough to shock thinking men and to disturb deeply — but not deeply enough to arouse all-out opposition — some of the more liberal forces within the Republican Party. The Republican liberals felt they had to go along with the retention of Goldwater as the Senatorial campaign chairman, largely because his big-money backing made it impolitic for them to do anything else, but when Goldwater tried to force his way into the inner councils of the party's top directorate, the liberals balked and firmly closed the door.

After the defeat of 1960, the Republicans created a leadership conference, composed of outstanding party leaders in both houses of Congress. The party's national chairman presided over the conference, and its minority leaders, Senator Dirksen and Rep. Charles A. Halleck, of Indiana, were its principal members, the stars of its so-called "Ev and Charlie" television show. Goldwater felt that he should be a member of this inner circle, with a chance to impress his arch-conservative views on the party's leaders — and perhaps to win the boon of an occasional television appearance with Ev and Charlie.

Goldwater's good friend, Senator Styles Bridges, of New Hampshire, backed him in his aspiration and broached the subject at a meeting of the leadership conference. At once, strong opposition developed. Senator Thomas H. Kuchel, of California, a Republican liberal deeply disturbed by the prairie-fire spread of Radical Rightism in his state, said flatly that he didn't think it was wise to give Goldwater a new forum. Equally opposed to the idea were Senators Jacob K. Javits, of New York, and Clifford P. Case, of New Jersey. Goldwater, rebuffed, was persistent. He made a direct appeal to Dirksen, but though Dirksen was friendly, the result was the same. The liberals had had to accept Goldwater as campaign chairman, but they weren't going to open the door any wider to the furtherance of his ambitions.

Goldwater himself kept those ambitions well-cloaked under a pose of seeming modesty and indifference. He was, he often said, just "pooping around" the edges of this Presidential thing. He had backers across the country; they were enthusiastic; and they had started this draft-Goldwater business. There really wasn't much he could do about it, now, was there? Sometimes, he indicated he didn't think he had a chance, he wasn't really taking the thing seriously; sometimes, he seemed to give listeners the impression that he would really prefer to stay as Senator from Arizona. It all tended to play down any hint of real purpose, a purpose that from the record would seem to have been born in the fires of 1960; it was like a possum-play, designed to lull the eastern liberals into the belief that Barry himself didn't mean it — and so they didn't have to worry.

One who wasn't deceived at the time was Gore Vidal. The young liberal playwright, himself a native of Washington and long familiar with the Washington scene, wrote an article in *Life* June 9, 1961 under the title "A Liberal Meets Mr. Conservative." In this, Vidal quite accurately judged the seriousness of Goldwater's intentions. In one significant passage, Vidal asked Goldwater what *he* would do if *he* were ever elected President.

"On the word 'President,'" Vidal wrote, "I noticed a faint flush of the fever. His eyes glittered. He sat back in his chair. 'If I was President,' he began with a new weight and authority, 'I'd move slowly, cautiously at first. You'd have to feel your pathway. Not that my ideas are new ideas. No, they're old, old ideas.'"

He talked of politics, of the ways political parties are born and molded.

Vidal wrote, quoting Goldwater:

"'. . . A political party can only start around a strong individual.' He looked past me at the bust [of Lincoln] on the mantelpiece; his jaw had set. 'Like Lincoln. The people were there looking for a party, looking for this strong individual. And there he was and that's how the Republican Party started. A strong individual.'

"The next question was obvious. Was Goldwater that 'strong individual?' Could he lead his people out of the wilderness? Were there enough of them to allow him to re-create that dream of Eden conservatives evoke whenever they recall the bright simple days of our old agrarian republic? But I let it go. Neither of us knew the answer. He had his hopes, and that was enough."

All the time, behind the façade of Goldwater's public indifference, powerful and extremely busy beavers were at work. Only faint hints of these behind-the-scenes endeavors found their way into the eastern press, and these were generally overlooked, generally ignored. Looking back, it becomes obvious that they should not have been; that they represented the first signs of serious and determined purpose.

One of the most significant spoors on the trail to the 1964 nomination was left on December 1 and 2, 1962 when a group of some fifty to sixty wealthy and politically influential backers gathered in a motel on Michigan Avenue in Chicago. The bulk of the delegates were from the South, Midwest and West, with just a few strays from the East; and they were all united in purpose — to block the nomination of Nelson Rockefeller, a Republican liberal, and to insure the selection of Barry Goldwater by the party convention in 1964.

One of the participants told newsmen afterward that those attending pledged $250,000, the nucleus of a $3 million campaign fund. Others said cautiously — and perhaps evasively — that no such fancy figure had been mentioned. Barry Goldwater, home in Phoenix, insisted he had no idea what it was all about.

Significantly, however, some of the persons present at this 1962 gathering in Chicago were to become key cogs in the Goldwater machine in its drive to the 1964 nomination, and the strategy mapped here was the one that was followed to victory — a strategy that relied on a heavy phalanx of Goldwater votes in the South, the Midwest and the Rocky Mountain States.

Among those present at this Chicago draft-Goldwater session were these key figures:

Cliff White, a New York public relations man long active in politics; a key operative in raising funds and infiltrating Republican delegations to capture votes for Goldwater in the final months of the 1964 drive to the nomination.

Wirt A. Yerger, Jr., Mississippi State Republican chairman, and Peter O'Donnell, Jr., Texas State Republican chairman, both strongly influential in putting together a practically Solid South for Goldwater at the 1964 convention.

William Rusher, of the *National Review*, often credited with being one of the major architects of the Goldwater strategy that contemplates victory through an amalgamation of the votes of the racist South, the agrarian Midwest and Southwest, plus a successful foray into several big states like California and Illinois.

Robert Morris, former counsel for the Senate Internal Security Committee, later legal representative for Maj. Gen.

Edwin A. Walker, who was cashiered from his command in Europe for indoctrinating his troops with Radical Right propaganda.

Charles Barr, of Chicago, executive of the Standard Oil Company of Indiana; Jeremiah Milbank, well-known New York financier; and Edmund Lynch, Jr., of the New York office of the brokerage firm of Merrill, Lynch, Pierce, Fenner & Smith, one of the largest brokerage houses in the nation — the experts on the delicate task of raising the kind of millions needed to finance an all-out campaign for the Presidency.

These and others like them were the men who met in Chicago in 1962 to get the Goldwater bandwagon off and rolling. Their purpose was clearly stated by Yerger.

"We're the conservative party," he said, "and we've got to have a conservative candidate if we expect to win."

The drive to insure the selection of this conservative candidate gathered momentum in April, 1963, when the National Draft Goldwater Committee was formally organized. It was headed by one of the Chicago conferees, Peter O'Donnell, Jr., the Texas Republican Chairman. At the same time, the propaganda drums began to beat on a variety of fronts. The *Arizona Daily Star* ran editorials saying it would be perfectly legal and proper, despite what Goldwater had said about Lyndon Johnson in 1960, for Goldwater to run for both the Presidency and re-election to the Senate. The *Star*, commenting on April 22 that "the Goldwater Presidential star continued to grow brighter," reported that the Senator had been the guest of honor at a large $100-a-plate dinner in Phoenix and that he was to be the featured guest at a $1,000-a-plate party gathering in Washington on May 9. This latter dinner, attended by some 400 GOP regulars, ostensibly was held to honor all Republican Senators, but the program was so arranged that the spotlight was on just one Senator.

All the evidence clearly suggests that a power play of major proportions was being organized; but Goldwater, who had announced his availability even before Nixon was defeated, still pretended surprise and reluctance. He kept insisting "this draft thing started without my knowledge" and that "I never sought this position." He did not, he said, know exactly what he was going to do about it. One would have to be extremely credulous to believe this. All the time Goldwater was protesting, the Birchers and their co-workers were infiltrating party organizations in mountain states like Montana and Wyoming, and they were laying their plans to raid the huge California Republican organization. And even though Goldwater continued to enact the role of the reluctant dragon, he had already rented all 51 rooms on the 15th floor of the Mark Hopkins Hotel in San Francisco for the period of the 1964 Republican convention. This, certainly, was a sign of political affluence — and determined intent.

On the level of practical politics, a comprehensive battle plan was also drafted at this time. It was based originally on the assumption that President Kennedy would be the 1964 Democratic nominee, and it counted heavily, as Goldwater was to continue to count, on the civil rights backfire in the South. The author of the plan was William Rusher, of the *National Review*, another of the original Chicago conferees. After the Nixon defeat in 1960, Rusher had prepared a widely circulated confidential memorandum suggesting that die-hard conservatives sit on their hands and wait for the liberals of both parties to bring ruin to the country. Then the people would be looking for a messiah — and the far right would have its chance. But by the spring of 1963, Rusher had changed his mind. He produced a mass-distributed pamphlet designed to demonstrate that Goldwater could win in '64 without the big Northeastern and Central industrial states, simply by welding together the votes of the South and West. Rusher ascribed the 1960 defeat to Nixon's moderation (Goldwater's view precisely) and held out the hope that Goldwater could cash in on a vast but persistently silent conservative vote that had sulked at home because of the steady succession of "me-too" candidates.

Bruce Chapman, publisher of *Advance,* a Republican progressive magazine, ridiculed the contents of the Rusher memos. There was, he said, a silent right wing majority that "is indeed underground and not voting; it is dead — in body and in ballot." He pointed out that Nixon himself had attributed his defeat to his failure to appeal to Negroes and urban voters, and he suggested that the far right was "now re-writing history" and that, if it kept at the task long enough, it might succeed in "turning history on its head." As for Goldwater's persistent appeals for party unity, Chapman said, in words that were to have special meaning in 1964: "When Barry Goldwater calls for unity in the Republican Party, it's like an arsonist calling for the fire department."

In this year of 1963, there was one surface development so revealing of the Goldwater mind and attitude that it must be mentioned. This was Goldwater's stand on Kennedy's nuclear test-ban treaty with Russia.

The treaty, which banned nuclear testing in the atmosphere and so promised to bring an end to the rain of radioactive fallout that was polluting the habitat of man, was widely hailed as a boon to humankind and a sign of the possible easing of Cold War tensions. Goldwater announced at the outset that he was going to be "open-minded" about the treaty, but his open-minded phase did not last much longer than overnight. Soon he was proposing a condition — that the treaty should not become effective until the Russians moved all their troops out of Cuba. Simultaneously, in a speech in Madison, Wisconson, that opened a window on his mind, he declared that he was against "peaceful co-existence as the Russians use the term" because it is equivalent to "giving tyranny a protected sanctuary from which it can erode or attack freedom."

These twin strands seemed to many to put Goldwater in the foremost ranks of the war-bent. He was, in essence, against the test-ban that might ease world tensions, and in the same breath he was denouncing "peaceful co-existence." As the conservative Washington *Evening Star* pointed out, the Russians "already have their protected sanctuary. Is Senator Goldwater advocating a war to drive them out?"

Goldwater's suggestion that we use the test-ban as a trading device was so half-baked that it brought denunciations from all quarters. Even Sen. Gordon Allott (R., Colo.), who usually saw eye-to-eye with Goldwater, abandoned him. Senator Javits said Goldwater's scheme would "open up all the questions involved in the Cold War," with each side matching the other with demands for concessions that would continue ad infinitum. Senator Mike Mansfield, of Montana, the Democratic Majority Leader, called the proposal "a mischievous toying with the health and the hopes of the people of the U.S." And Senator Hubert Humphrey (D., Minn.) denounced the Goldwater plan as representing not constructive policy, but "partisan mischief."

Even editorialists of normally conservative papers like the Baltimore *Sun* and the Washington *Star* backed Humphrey. The *Sun* pointed out that, if we imposed a Cuban condition, the Russians might insist we get out of Iran; if we said all right, we might — provided the Russians got out of East Berlin — the dickering could go on endlessly and futilely. As the Washinton *Star* said, there would be "an absolute stalemate."

Goldwater responded to the barrage of criticism, as he almost always does, by elevating himself to a lofty plateau of principle, adopting the pose of a man who courageously is going to stand by his beliefs even if they cause his political death. Whether Goldwater himself believes this is a moot point. The real fact is that the pose enables him to put the gloss of high purpose on stands that frequently conflict with popular opinion, but almost invariably agree with the fanatically held tenets of the Radical Right.

In the Senate on Sept. 19, 1963 Goldwater announced he would vote against the test-ban treaty in these words:

"I do not vote against the hope of peace, but only against the illusion of it. I do not vote for war, but for the strength to prevent it. . . .

"I have been told that to vote against this treaty is to commit political suicide.

"I will vote against this treaty because in my heart, mind, soul and conscience I feel it detrimental to the strength of my country.

"If it means political suicide to vote for my country and against this treaty, then I commit it gladly. It is not my future that concerns me. It is my country — and what my conscience tells me is how best I may serve it."

On Sept. 23, 1963 the Senate rejected his Cuban reservation resolution by a vote of 75 to 17 and went on to ratify the test-ban treaty. No stigma should attach, of course, to a man who stands by his beliefs despite the weight of the opposition. Such stands, conscientiously taken, merit only praise. But it has to seem significant that Goldwater, who preaches the doctrine of freedom and liberty and individualism, stands always in the corner of power, blind to the higher hopes and aspirations of men; blind and obdurate even when virtually all around him can see the higher goal. His is always and unfailingly, except in the interests of wealth and military force and aggressiveness, a policy of negativism.

CHAPTER XVI

The Issue Is Drawn

Virtually alone among the leaders of his party, Gov. Nelson A. Rockefeller saw early and with clarity the great looming issue of the 1964 campaign — an un-American extremism. In a statement on July 15, 1963, though he carefully refrained from mentioning Goldwater by name, he called for a clear repudiation of the tactics Goldwater's followers had adopted in the West — tactics that, Rockefeller said, "would not only defeat the Republican Party in 1964 but would destroy it."

Rockefeller based his surprise attack on the manner in which the ultras, just the previous month, had engineered the takeover of the Young Republican National Convention in San Francisco.

"The proceedings were dominated by extremist groups, carefully organized, well-financed and operating through the tactics of ruthless, roughshod intimidation," Rockefeller said. He added: "These are the tactics of totalitarianism."

Rockefeller saw great danger for the entire party from "the vociferous and well-drilled extremist elements" who were "embarked on a determined and ruthless effort to take over the party, its platform and its candidates" — an almost perfect description, exactly twelve months in advance of the actual event, of developments at the Republican National Convention in San Francisco in mid-July, 1964.

Goldwater's strategy of basing Republican hopes of victory upon a Southern-Midwestern coalition, writing off the most populous states in the nation, also shocked Rockefeller. He called it "absolutely incredible." It would transform the GOP from a national into a sectional force, he declared; it would leave the party of Lincoln with a program "based on racism and sectionalism."

Rockefeller's furious attack stunned Republicans, and

there was at the time much skepticism about the purity of his motives. Until quite recently, Rockefeller had been considered the front-runner in the race for his party's nomination, and during this period, he had appeared to be trying to blur the image of his liberalism by making attacks on the Democrats that seemed almost Goldwaterish in tone. He had also made a visible effort to achieve a rapproachment with Goldwater, inviting the Arizona Senator to breakfast on several occasions at the Rockefeller Foxhall Road estate in Washington. All signs had pointed to a cordiality between the two that might result in the amicable bridging of the widening chasm between the Republican Party's left and right flanks. Then had come Rockefeller's controversial remarriage to the recently divorced Mrs. Margaretta (Happy) Murphy, the mother of four small children. The Rockefeller image lost its luster; his standing in the public opinion polls plummeted; and Goldwater spurted to the fore for the first time. It was at this precise juncture that Rockefeller hurled his first bomb into the Goldwater camp.

Many thought at the time that the New York Governor was merely indulging in a cheap political tactic to refurbish his liberal image, but time was to show that such interpretations did him a grave injustice. Rockefeller's consistent and gritty performance for the next year, right down to the moment when an organized claque tried to hoot him off the platform at San Francisco, seemed to say that this was indeed a matter of principle with him; that he, almost alone among the major leaders of his party, had seen the face of the Radical Right and recognized the evil it represented. What was it that Rockefeller had seen?

He had seen primarily the storm-trooper tactics that had been ruthlessly employed in the takeover of the Young Republicans at San Francisco. Delegates to that affair later gave Rowland Evans and Robert Novak, of the New York *Herald-Tribune,* vivid eyewitness accounts of the power putsch that had steamrollered all opposition.

Allan C. Young, of North Dakota, after "sadly" reporting "that there are extremists in our party," said: ". . . the whole convention at times was rocked by screaming, yelling, wild-eyed young men and women who would accept order only after they had their way regardless of the majority will."

Dale M. Hiller, of Delaware, put it this way: ". . . a group of people . . . came with the deliberate and openly admitted purpose of obstructing and disrupting proceedings . . . they form a force with which the Young Republicans and the whole Republician Party will have to reckon. We have seen them in action. We know."

Even Pro-Goldwater delegates, if they showed any inclination to condemn such tactics, were promptly read out of the lodge and branded as being somehow tainted with the virus of liberalism. The New Jersey delegation, most of them for Goldwater, was attacked as being "liberal." Mrs. Taffy Goldsmith, of Dallas, Tex., a conservative and a Goldwater booster ever since 1956, couldn't stomach the Birchers' strong-arm methods and tried to buck them. When she returned home, she found that a whispering campaign had been started to discredit her as a crypto-liberal. Birchers demanded that she resign as a national committeewoman and told her she wasn't wanted in the draft-Goldwater campaign. As Evans and Novak wrote, these and other experiences made it clear that the extremists were determined to seize control and to keep it in the hands of "a disciplined elite," a dictatorial elite that would have no use for dissenting Taffy Goldsmiths.

These "totalitarian" tactics, as Rockefeller so accurately described them, had been on display in California for several months. The "mean and dirty" methods advocated by Robert Welch as perfectly appropriate for the holy war against liberalism had been employed with a vengeance by his young and fanatical Birchite followers. They staged systematic raids on local chapters of the GOP businessmen's organization known as the California Republican Assembly (CRA). When a CRA meeting was to be held, a group of young Birchers would get together, invade the premises, shout and yell and throw things until they were made members of the club. Then they would take over, sometimes walking out with the club's records and checkbook.

In January, 1963, by the use of such tactics, the Birchers swallowed the California Young Republican Federation lock, stock and barrel. They forced their way into local YR groups, padded their rolls with new Birchite members — and draped the dangerous tag of "liberal" on all who tried to stop them. Some Birch chapters simply constituted themselves Young Republican clubs. When moderate Young Republicans spoke out against the "power grab" of the Birchers, they found themselves the butts of typically McCarthyite innuendoes. Why, one older Bircher asked darkly in the press, should they fear "the intrusion and infiltration of constitutional Americanism?" The inevitable dead-end of McCarthyism was expressed in such developments; it was a creed of smear and intimidation aimed, not just at its avowed object, Communists, but at liberals, at conservatives who opposed the fanatics, at anyone who disagreed. And, in California, there was no stopping it. The Birchers grabbed control of the state Young Republican organization and installed their hand-picked candidate as president — young, wealthy, fanatical Robert Gaston, of Los Angeles, from whom more was to be heard later.

Such was the record, clear and undeniable, that backed up the Rockefeller charges. Goldwater's first reaction was one of silence. So Rockefeller attacked again. Five days after he had issued his first statement, he gave the press another, calling upon Goldwater by name to kick out the "lunatic fringe" that was backing his candidacy. Rockefeller insisted that Goldwater must disavow the extremists "for his own good and the good of his party" or wind up a "captive candidate" of "the John Birchers and others like them." What Rockefeller did not understand, what few Republicans were willing to acknowledge, was that Goldwater would never disown the movement because he was ideologically and to some extent organizationally a part of it.

Despite the Rockefeller charges which posed a definite challenge to him, despite the well-established record of the rowdy tactics being used by his followers in California, Goldwater persisted with the obdurateness of the purposely blind. He played the same old record, refusing to recognize that there even was a Radical Right, trying to transfer the onus of radicalism to the liberal left. In a news conference in New York on July 29, 1963, he said this:

"I'm more concerned about the Americans for Democratic Action who are in Government and who advocate centralization of Government than any right society members who are not in Government. I don't spend my time worrying about conservative and too-conservative. I worry about the radical left in Government."

This mid-July of 1963 was a rough period for Goldwater. He was rocked in his own party by Rockefeller's charges of extremism, and at the Governor's Conference in Miami, Gov. Edmund (Pat) Brown, of California, the man who had buried Richard Nixon in the 1962 gubernatorial contest, swung a haymaker at Goldwater, accusing him of being a segregationist. The charge touched off a day-long dispute among the governors at the conference on the theme: Was or wasn't Goldwater a segregationist? One Southern governor who might be expected to know, Gov. Carl E. Sanders, of Georgia, a Democrat, agreed with Pat Brown by saying that he thought Goldwater "to a certain extent" was a segregationist.

These charges brought roars of outrage from Goldwater. Brown, he said, had been speaking "from his usual source of ignorance," and he insisted that the questions about where he stood on segregation "had been answered before they were asked." Goldwater pointed indignantly to his own role in desegregating the Arizona Air National Guard, the Phoenix municipal airport, the Phoenix schools. Why, he said, he had actually belonged at one time to the National Association for the Advancement of Colored People, and he had even on one occasion contributed $400 to the NAACP. This was all true. There can be little doubt that Goldwater personally has never displayed a drop of racial prejudice; but, at the same time, there can be just as little doubt that, as a practical politician, he has played with the issue in the most irresponsible and demagogic fashion.

He had denounced the Supreme Court's desegregation ruling. He had criticized the use of federal troops to quell the riots in Little Rock, Arkansas. And for years he had been preaching a sermon dear to the hearts of the Southern white supremacists — the philosophy of states' rights, an issue that was supposed to have been settled by the Civil War a century earlier. States' rights, if adopted in Goldwater's extreme form as a national policy, inevitably would give the Southern white politicians and their followers absolute freedom to run their own peculiar institutions in their own peculiar way, maintaining segregation and keeping the Negro in his appointed lowly place until the end of time. Though not an intellectual man, Goldwater couldn't have been so stupid as not to recognize this, but in his callous play for Southern votes and Southern support, he had pandered to the prejudices and the passions of the white supremacists.

One of his more extreme performances had taken place at the Republican Southern States Regional Conference held in Atlanta, on November 18, 1961. In a press conference there, he had made a series of extreme statements that were to come back to haunt him. "I wouldn't like to see my party assume that it is the role of the Federal Government to enforce integration in the schools," he had said. Both parties had "made a mistake in trying to be specific about civil rights" in their platforms. At the Republican Convention in 1964, he pledged, "I would bend every muscle to see that the South has a voice on everything that affects the life of the South." And capping all, in regard to GOP strategy, he said this: "We're not going to get the Negro vote as a bloc in 1964 or 1968, so we ought to go hunting where the ducks are."

This last frank expression of demagogic purpose didn't read too well when Goldwater saw it in cold print; and when it was flung back in his face during the discussions at the Miami Governor's Conference in 1963, he almost blew a gasket. He had been misquoted, he shouted as always; he had never said any such thing. Richard Dudman, of the St. Louis *Post-Dispatch*, did a little research and reported that not only had all reporters at the Atlanta conference heard Goldwater say what he had said, but, even more conclusive, was the fact that Goldwater had evidently liked his words so much he had repeated them almost verbatim on a *Meet the Press* program the following day. Asked on the program if he had a winning prescription for Republicans, Goldwater had said: "I have a general formula, put in a way that I think most people will understand. If you are going hunting for ducks, you go where the ducks are. . . . I would concentrate, then, the Republican fire where we are strong: In the southern cities, in the smaller cities all across America, in the urban areas, in the country areas. . . ."

Despite Goldwater's sensitiveness on the segregation issue and his blindness on the Radical Right threat, the evidence continued to mount that he was the political darling of these two fanatical factions. It was a combination, again, that was reminiscent of the forces behind Hitler, wealthy ultra-conservatives fearful of liberal reforms that might jolt their tight little world joining hands with hate-filled racists in a most potent and dangerous combination. The union of the political Radical Right with the bigots showed clearly in the pattern of Goldwater endorsements. Robert Welch, of course, had always been for Goldwater. As far back as 1958, he had proclaimed in his *Blue Book*: "I know Barry fairly well. He is a great American. . . . He is absolutely superb in his Americanism. I'd love to see him President of the United States, and maybe someday we shall." In 1961, on *Meet the Press*, Welch had added: "I personally have been for Goldwater for President, for any great office." By the summer of 1963, *We, the People!* and some dozen other far-right organizations had joined the Goldwater legions. In Oklahoma City, the Rev. Billy James Hargis' Christian Crusade held its annual convention, indulging in a saturnalia of denunciation of the Kennedy family, the New Frontier, the State Department, "the National Association for the Agitation of Colored People," liberals, "dupes," Communists, the United Nations, the Supreme Court, Harvard, Alger Hiss, Dwight D. Eisenhower — and applauding to the echo every mention of Goldwater's name. And in Atlanta, the White Citizen's Council plastered Goldwater stickers on the walls of its meeting hall and made the hall itself vibrate with shouts.

In California, in September, 1963, Robert Gaston began to beat the bushes for Goldwater votes. The fanatical young man who had been catapulted into command of the state's Young Republicans by the Birchers' strong-arm methods erupted in a speech in Salinas in which, according to the San Francisco *Chronicle*, he "bitingly attacked most eminent Republicans and all Democrats." The Democrats, he shouted, were a parcel of "thieves, crooks, liars and trash."

Calling for all-out support of Goldwater's Presidential candidacy, Gaston admonished his listeners:

"If every one of you can't deliver a precinct for Goldwater, the only draft will be the one sweeping him off the convention floor. Talk to your neighbor — if he doesn't like it, ram it down his throat."

Gaston proclaimed that his objective was to create a Republican Party based on "principle." He did not of course define the ingredients of his principles, but then, actually, he didn't have to. They were apparent.

"We will take control of this party — and this nation," he declaimed.

Even for Goldwater, this was going a bit too far. Even he, if only momentarily, began to get some idea of what was involved in extremism, and he growled:

"Gaston had better keep his mouth shut or get out of active Republican politics. He is intemperate and doing great damage to the Young Republicans. Until he learns to respect the Democrats who are our opponents and not call them the vicious names he has called them; until he learns that in politics you don't cram anything down people's throats; until he learns that Eisenhower did not wreck the GOP, he had better keep his mouth shut."

The recognition was purely temporary. Not even the assassination of President Kennedy on that unforgettable day in Dallas, November 22, 1963, could give Barry Goldwater second thoughts about the dangers implicit in encouraging passion-arousing demagogues and ruthless advocates of violence, both dedicated to the pernicious thesis that the end justifies every means. Though Lee Harvey Oswald, charged with the murder of a much-beloved President, had been a leftist, many felt that the hate-filled, supercharged atmosphere of Dallas, the creation of the Radical Right, had supplied the final stimulus that triggered the explosion of his unstable personality. It was a personality that, when it flipped beyond the borderlines of rationality, wanted to kill — and it didn't much matter whom: the Birchite Maj Gen. Edwin A. Walker, at whom Oswald is said to have pegged a shot; or Richard Nixon, at whom, according to his wife, he wanted to shoot; or President Kennedy, whom, by all the evidence, he killed. The tragedy and martyrdom of Dallas would seem to say that you cannot go around the countryside shouting treason at every prominent American in sight, advocating violence and "mean and dirty" tactics, without triggering into homicidal mania just such psychotic characters as Lee Harvey Oswald. Logic says that, if the fanatics of the right and the hate-filled racists are to have their way, there is going to be more, and more horrible, violence.

But Barry Goldwater, the decent-seeming Phoenix Country Club McCarthy, could never admit this. The assassination of President Kennedy gave him some bad moments. Though political enemies, the two men, as Senators, had been friends. Each had charm to which the other responded, and there can be no doubt that Goldwater was as shocked as most Americans by the tragedy in Dallas.

On the political front, it seemed at first as if the Kennedy assassination might put an end to the Goldwater Presidential aspirations. The Rusher-drafted campaign strategy for 1964 had been based upon the supposition that Kennedy would be the opponent. With arch-conservatives in revolt against Kennedy liberalism, with the South up in arms over the Kennedy civil rights program, the blueprint calling for a welding of Southern white supremacism with Midwestern rural Republicanism and fanatical radical rightism had appeared to offer some prospects of success. But with Lyndon B. Johnson in the White House, the first Southerner to be President since the Civil War, the outlook was drastically changed. Johnson certainly would have a better chance of carrying the South, depriving Goldwater of this citadel of strength. For a time, it looked as if the Goldwater candidacy might collapse — but only for a time. President Johnson's forthright advocacy of a strong civil rights measure revived the hope that the racist-Radical Right combination might work. And Goldwater, except for his isolated slapdown of the fanatical Gaston, reverted to the astigmatism that prevented him from seeing that the Radical Right even existed.

By March of 1964, he was saying in Sacramento:

"This extremist thing is not worthy of discussion at any responsible level, unless it's the left-wing extremists who are in government. . . . Anybody who can't see the issues today has no business running for the Presidency. I just can't for the life of me see how extremism — as it has been explained to me — can have any bearing on the issues in this or any other state. I think that it's an issue of small minds."

The statement prompted the Sacramento *Bee* to take a look at the facts. Just the previous week, the newspaper said, Goldwater had "witnessed with his own eyes the take-over by his conservative followers" of the once-moderate California Republican Assembly. If Goldwater didn't know the Birchers were behind this putsch, as he had insisted, the *Bee* could see only this explanation: "As one Republican source commented he was blind or befuddled. It is hard to believe Goldwater is naive." The same GOP source, the *Bee* added, named a half-dozen members of the Birch Society who were active in the CRA takeover, and all Barry would have to do to acquaint himself with the facts, the paper declared, was to pick up some of the Radical Right propaganda that cluttered CRA headquarters during the meeting.

Goldwater, of course, was not risking any such self-education. A look at some of his more prominent backers might explain why. *Advance* tagged some of them in its January, 1964, issue. The National Draft Goldwater Committee, it said, was led by segregationists like Wirt Yerger and James Martin, the South Carolina rightist who almost won election to the U.S. Senate, both of them among the original 1962 conferees in Chicago. William Rusher, of the *National Review,* had been assigned to "the job of 'liaison' with the lunatic fringe — keep them working but quiet." *Advance* added: "John Birch leader N. B. Livingston, Jr., has taken the helm of Ohioans for Goldwater, while another Society stalwart, Kenneth G. Bentson, is treasurer of the Arizona Goldwater for President Committee. Coloradoans for Goldwater have as their president a leader in a group of far right doctors, led by Birchers, who broke away from the 'too liberal' AMA. Birch leader John Rousselot [once a Birchite Congressman] is continually addressing Goldwater meetings in California."

The long record said quite conclusively that Goldwater was no "captive candidate" of the Radical Right. This was a case where the captain, the officers and the crew were one.

CHAPTER XVII

The Primaries

The greatest problem faced by the Goldwater strategists in the primary campaigns of 1964 was to keep their candidate from opening his mouth and emitting words that he would later like to reach up, grab and eat. It proved, from first to last, to be an impossible task.

Goldwater had hardly announced his candidacy before he rushed headlong to stake out his claim as the Rich Man's Candidate of 1964. On January 15, 1964, just twelve days after he had pitched his hat into the ring in the press conference at his House on the Top of the Hill, he went before the Economic Club of New York and denounced President Johnson's "war on poverty."

The idea that poverty and unemployment are caused by lack of education "is like saying that people have big feet because they wear big shoes," Goldwater wisecracked. "The fact is that most people who have no skill have no education for the same reason — low intelligence or ambition."

The reaction to this flat declaration was one of shock on both sides of the political fence. Senator Abraham Ribicoff (D., Conn.), former Secretary of Health, Education and Welfare in the Kennedy cabinet, said mildly enough: "I cannot share the impression he leaves . . . that if only the unemployed would have the gumption to go to work, all our welfare problems would be solved." A liberal Republican Senator told *The New York Times*: "Some of Goldwater's statements are appalling — an embarrassment."

"Appalling" seems the right word. *The New York Times* found "an insensitivity" about such remarks delivered in the affluent atmosphere of the Economic Club. "The most charitable judgment about such pronouncements," it wrote, "is that Senator Goldwater really knows very little about the United States and its people. . . . He has evidently never visited the rat-infested slums of Harlem or the shanties in which migratory farm laborers have to live. He shows no knowledge of the problems of the Negro sharecropper in Mississippi, the Puerto Rican dishwasher in this city, the West Virginia coal miner thrown out of a job by automation. But ignorance is hardly a qualification for the post of the President of the United States. . . ."

Yet no one who had followed Goldwater's pronouncements over the years should have been greatly surprised. The quality of the man — his callousness to the lot of common people, his preoccupation almost exclusively with the selfish interests of his own well-placed class — had been demonstrated time and time again. A rapid-fire sequence of actions in 1961 vividly illustrated the point.

On March 16, 1961 he spoke before the Delaware Valley Industrial Editors at the Poor Richard Club. He had a prescription that he thought the Kennedy Administration should follow to end the recession. It consisted of two main parts: withdrawal of the recommendation to hike the minimum wage from $1 to $1.25 an hour (Barry hated like sin to see the workingman getting that extra quarter); and granting hefty tax cuts to big business — liberalizing the tax depletion allowance, as Barry put it — to "throw the economy into high gear and reduce unemployment in a matter of days."

On May 8, 1961 Barry swooped into Flint, Michigan, and here the Desert Don Quixote, the foe of bigness, came out solidly for bigness as long as it was bigness in business. We must choose, he proclaimed, between big business and big government. The evidence he cited for this choice was the manned suborbital space shot recently achieved by the United States. Small business, he said, could never have accomplished such a technological advance. This demonstrated to Goldwater that there was only one choice, "big business or a much bigger government," and in making a decision between the two, "we must no longer ask ourselves whether an industrial organization is too big, but rather is it big enough to do the job." Only an especially obtuse man, or one utterly blinded by his own peculiar preudices, would ever have cited the suborbital shot — a project financed, masterminded and carried to fruition by big government — as the clinching evidence for the virtues of big industry. Equally revealing was the fact that Goldwater, in propounding his flat either-or proposition, appeared never to have heard of the middle way practiced by so many of the economies of Western Europe. (Gore Vidal had reported he acknowledged he knew little about European socialism and economics.) It seemed never to occur to him that big government and big business — and big labor — could join in a mutually beneficial partnership, as they had in so much of the Western community of nations. The narrowness of the mind nurtured in the Rotary and business clubs of Phoenix stood self-revealed.

All of these performances in 1961 had been capped, however, in mid-July by Goldwater's enthusiastic endorsement of the action of City Manager Joseph McD. Mitchell, of Newburgh, N.Y. , in announcing a crackdown on the city's welfare program. Mitchell announced he wasn't going to pay relief funds to mothers of children born out of wedlock, and he was going to eliminate "chiselers" — they would work or else. He clearly implied that Newburgh was being victimized by a lot of transient workers (the implication was that most were Negroes) who were sponging off the city.

Though it wasn't clear under the Mitchell get-tough program just what would happen to children who had the misfortune to have unwed mothers, Goldwater promptly rushed forward, shouting hosannahs. He met with Mitchell in Washington and described his reaction afterward as that of "one American's admiration for another to protect my taxes." Goldwater added: "I don't like to see my taxes paid for children born out of wedlock. I'm tired of professional chiselers walking up and down the street who don't work and have no intention of working."

The facts, as uncovered by subsequent investigation, shed a decidedly different light on these suppositions. It developed that, of the 900 persons on the Newburgh relief rolls, there was only one who could have worked a 40-hour week. And he was white, an unemployed steel worker, a native of Newburgh, whose wife was in the hospital and who was taking care of five children at home. Mitchell's much-ballyhooed drive against the supposed army of chiselers collapsed; he eventually resigned as city manager; and it is perhaps of some significance that he has popped up in 1964 as an executive in the ranks of the Southern segregationists.

This record tells much about the Presidential candidate who took off for New Hampshire in early January, 1964, to expose himself for the first time to the voters, with a truly national spotlight focused upon him. It is a strange circumstance, but true, that a man like Goldwater may spend years, fly hundreds of thousands of miles, make thousands of speeches, write a newspaper column and books — and still remain something of an unknown quantity to the majority of voters. The reason for this paradox is doubtless to be found in the awesome powers and responsibilities of the Presidency itself. It is one thing for a U.S. Senator from Arizona to explode in vituperation against Walter Reuther, to want to sell TVA and dismantle much of the federal government; Senators say a lot of things, not all of them sensible. But it is decidedly different when a man who aspires to be President says the same things and acts in the same way. Instinctively, the people are judging the man in a new frame of reference, deciding in their own minds how he measures up to the image they have of the Presidency and the crushing burdens the man who fills that office must bear. The mere fact of Goldwater's seeking this lonely pinnacle of power would shed a new light on him — and on everything he did and said. How, in this new light, would he look to the voters?

Goldwater had everything going for him in New Hampshire. It was a strongly Republican state, a strongly conservative state. The ground, it appeared, was fertile for his gospel, and he had in addition the most powerful and influential backing a man could have. U.S. Senator Norris Cotton, New Hampshire's own, was masterminding his campaign; the State Republican organization had wholeheartedly endorsed him; and the major officeholders in the state graced his slate of delegates.

But Goldwater had hardly entered the state before he opened his mouth and began putting up into the frigid ozone words that might better have been eaten. On January 8, in a speech in Manchester, he urged that the NATO commander in Europe, General Lyman Lemnitzer, be given authority to use tactical nuclear weapons without the approval of the White House. Goldwater didn't tell his New Hampshire audiences that many of today's "tactical" nuclear weapons are more devastating than the bomb that was dropped on Hiroshima, but the suggestion that the responsibility for triggering a nuclear war should be entrusted to a general, who might be much more inclined to hasty decision and rash action than the President in the White House, began to make a lot of voters shudder.

Apparently unaware of the reaction he had started, Goldwater went right on. On the same day that he proposed giving the NATO commander the power to push the nuclear button, he called in a speech in Concord for a new invasion of Cuba by Cuban exiles trained and supplied by the U.S. — and this time with air cover Goldwater would be "inclined" to give them.

The next day, January 9, in Portsmouth, Goldwater blasted Secretary of Defense McNamara and civilians in the Pentagon, whom, he said again, as he had said earlier, he feared more than the military. "I don't feel safe at all about our missiles, to tell you the truth," he said. "I wish the Defense Department could tell the American people how undependable the missiles in our silos actually are."

This unsupported and unsubstantiated charge caused an enormous flap. McNamara fired off a barrage at Goldwater, calling his statement "completely misleading, politically irresponsible and damaging to the national security." In the resulting uproar, the consensus seemed to be that our missiles are reliable. Rep. Carl Vinson (D., Ga), veteran chairman of the House Armed Services Committee, said no one contends they would go off (after all, the engines of manned bombers malfunction, too), but a heavy percentage of them would lift from their pads and fly straight and true to their targets. Even former President Eisenhower had to repudiate Goldwater. "I am confident we have just as good missiles as there are in the world," Ike told a Republican rally in Detroit.

Undeterred by this setback, Goldwater rushed onward and upward with more and fancier saber-rattling. When Fidel Castro turned off the water supplying the U.S. Naval Base at Guantanamo, Goldwater blew his stack. In a speech in Derry, New Hampshire, he proclaimed that we should "march out with a detachment of marines and turn it on ourselves." As the crowd cheered, Goldwater cried: "Our flag can be spat upon and torn to the ground, and as an American I'm sick and tired of it. I think I can promise President Johnson the backing of the American people if we don't take this one lying down."

In Havana, Castro taunted that, if the U.S. "tries to lay its hands on our water sources, we will fight to the last man and let Barry Goldwater know it. He should be in the first line of invaders."

Goldwater replied with another salvo. Marching the marines against Castro, it developed, really wasn't enough for him. In Washington on February 9, he again advocated a Cuban invasion, and this time he added another embellishment — he proposed we should use our power to put our allies, Great Britain and France, in their proper places. Britain was selling buses to Castro, and France was also trading with the bewhiskered Cuban. Goldwater wanted to use U.S. warships to halt such trading and turn back the vessels of our allies. He didn't seem to think Britain and France would take any particular umbrage at this, and as for what might happen if we invaded Cuba, he cavalierly ignored the fact that Russia had pledged to come to the aid of Castro. "It might lead to some shooting in Cuba. That's all," Barry said.

Waxing shriller with every speech, Goldwater stormed into McNamara's home territory on March 25, and in a speech before the Economic Club of Detroit, he unleashed an attack so savage that it stunned a large part of his conservative audience. He called McNamara "an adding machine warrior," who with his "whiz kids" and computers was giving America only "ledger sheet leadership."

"I fear for the suicide of my country," Goldwater cried. He added that, if McNamara had been defense secretary in the last century, "we'd still be relying on sailing ships." The Detroit *News* reported that many of those who heard Goldwater thought that he was "whey."

In New Hampshire, canny Yankee voters were weighing these performances. They were also digesting a number of Goldwater domestic pronouncements. New Hampshire is a poor state, and it ranks fourth in the nation in the number of elderly among its population. It was hardly a state in which to suggest that the Social Security system should be dismantled. Yet Goldwater did just about that. In one of his first speeches in Concord and repeatedly afterward, he told his audiences that he would change Social Security to make participation "voluntary." Governor Rockefeller promptly charged that such a change would "wreck the Social Security system," as indeed it would.

It quickly became apparent that Goldwater, with his own lungs, was bellowing himself into a pit of trouble in the Granite State. His deepening problems stemmed from two main sources: his own rapid-fire, nerve-shattering, hip-shooting performance on every warlike issue under the sun; and the obvious fact that he didn't know the state or its people—and he hadn't taken the trouble to learn. As a friend once said: "Barry's whole attitude has always been: 'Let somebody else take care of the details.'" Unfortunately, a President (or a man who is Presidential timber) must have the details in his own head. He must know. This failure to know was glaring in Goldwater. As Mary McGrory of the Washington *Evening Star* commented on March 5, Goldwater after nearly two months of campaigning "has yet to give a statistic about New Hampshire. He does not even trouble to mention the name of the town in which he finds himself."

She described in some detail Goldwater's appearance at Keene State College. He appeared ignorant of the fact that many of the students "were lean and hungry hill folk who worked hard for their education," and he talked to them "as if they were attending some country club college and had convertibles and pocket money to burn." When the meeting was thrown open to questions, the students wanted to know why Goldwater voted against federal aid to education. He replied weakly that he had voted for some of it, but that he'd voted against the vocational education bill because it contained more money than the President had asked for and because the people in Arizona told him they were getting more than they could use.

"There was an angry buzzing in the audience," Mary McGrory wrote. "A girl's voice rode out over it: 'Let them send it to New Hampshire,' she called out, and there was applause."

Goldwater obviously hadn't known that money was so scarce at Keene the students had recently marched 55 miles to the state capital seeking help. But worse was to come. The Keene students grilled Goldwater on his desire to scrap the federal relief program, and the Senator, evidently annoyed that his answers weren't eliciting the rousing cheers they did in Arizona, snapped: "Do you know anyone who is living in such abject poverty they are miserable?"

Mary McGrory wrote:

"There was an angry gasp in the audience. The boy said yes he did.

" 'Have any of you tried to help them?' asked the Senator, sure of his ground.

"Later, simmering students told reporters that there is a group of Catholic and Protestant club members who travel over the state helping the poor. Responding to a series of editorials about inhumane welfare procedures in the local paper, they have begged paper and paint from local merchants and go about refurbishing the homes of the needy."

Such was the Goldwater performance in New Hampshire. As the campaign dragged along, reporters on the scene could sense the initial Goldwater enthusiasm draining away and congealing at times into enmity. Thomas Walsh, a Colebrook attorney and former Republican County Chairman, told the Washington *Star*: "Rockefeller's been making Goldwater sound like an ass on these issues. I'm a conservative, and naturally I'd like to see Barry do well, but he's going downhill." A private poll of Republican voters, taken in early March, reflected alarm over the extreme stands Goldwater had taken. Typical comments were: "Goldwater is erratic. He would get us into war in no time." "He's the bomb-shelter candidate." "No matter what has been done, he's against it."

The result, when the New Hampshire voters went to the polls, was an emphatic verdict of disenchantment. Governor Rockefeller's divorce and remarriage had damaged him irreparably with the conservative New Hampshire electorate; but Goldwater's hip-shooting had done equally irreparable damage to himself. In this first test of Presidential stature, he had shown himself sadly wanting in the poise, the command of facts, the calmness and the balance people instinctively seek in their President. The voters of New Hampshire endorsed a candidate they hadn't seen or heard, one who was far away on the other side of the world — the handsome Henry Cabot Lodge, our Ambassador in South Vietnam.

A debacle of such magnitude almost certainly would have killed off the Presidential aspirations of any man but Goldwater. The emphatic "no" rendered at the polls by the voters of the Granite State led many, in the first flush of analysis, to conclude that even Goldwater had been done in. But such speculation reckoned without two special and very potent underlying factors. Goldwater still had influence where it counted, with the state and county chairmen of his party across the nation. In his years of ceaseless campaigning as Republican Senatorial Campaign Committee Chairman, he had done them infinite favors; he had packed in the crowds at their fund-raising dinners. They owed him. Furthermore, he now had the backing of the most fanatical force on the American political scene, the Birchers and their Radical Right brethren. Committed to Goldwater one and all, they had wangled or bulled their way into positions of influence in many a state committee; and so, when the time came to pick convention delegates from their several states, they were in a position to see that dedicated Goldwater men were chosen. The result was that, quietly, behind the scenes, despite the public setback in New Hampshire, the Goldwater drive pressed full steam ahead, with henchmen like the wily Cliff White sometimes spending twenty hours a day on the telephone, wheedling, browbeating, cajoling. Delegate by delegate and state by state, the votes fell into

Goldwater's lap and steadily swelled his hard-core strength until, without risking another public test at the polls, he stood within arm's reach of the nomination.

There remained just two primary hurdles—one in Oregon on May 15; the other, and the all-important one, in California, on June 2. A loss in Oregon would not be fatal; but California, with its huge bloc of 86 delegates, meant the vinegar works. Goldwater took a long, hard look at Oregon and, quite early, wrote it off. Henry Cabot Lodge was strong there, as Goldwater himself initially had been in New Hampshire, and Nelson Rockefeller was waging a strenuous campaign. Goldwater, though he put up a stiff rear-guard action, obviously had decided to let them fight it out and to concentrate his hunting "where the ducks were"—in the Radical Right purlieus of populous Southern California where Goldwaterism was almost like a religious faith.

In the eastern wing of the Republican Establishment, in much of the eastern press and in intellectual circles, there was an unshakable and fateful miasma of disbelief. The prevailing mood was that Goldwater, as a Presidential candidate, was just too incredible; the threat he posed *couldn't* be serious; *he* just *couldn't* get the nomination. Some fortuitous last-minute circumstance, some divine intervention would occur to block him.

It seemed for one fleeting moment that this, indeed, might be the case. Rockefeller in Oregon pulled as great an upset as Henry Cabot Lodge had in New Hampshire. Campaigning furiously, organizing in every county of the state, he overcame Lodge's lead and walked off with Oregon's 18 delegates to the national convention. The eastern Establishment sat back and sighed with relief. Rockefeller himself might not be able to get the nomination, but his upset victory in Oregon had given him needed momentum. Surely, now, he would be able to stop Goldwater in California.

This was too complacent an assumption. California, always an unpredictable state politically, posed serious problems. Just two candidates were entered in the California primary, Goldwater and Rockefeller, and it was evident from the start that this would be a head-butting contest that would virtually decide Goldwater's fate. In Goldwater's favor were some vital statistics. The large northern regions of the state, where Goldwaterism was less virulent than in the South, were less densely populated. Only some 40 percent of the state's electorate lives and votes here; some 60 percent, on the other hand, are concentrated in the southern counties, around

Los Angeles, where the Birchite virus kept the public temper in a constant ferment. These figures meant that Rockefeller was strongest, Goldwater weakest, in the sections of the state that counted least in the final tabulation of votes. Given this edge, Goldwater did what he always does: he went hunting where the ducks were; he concentrated everything in the South.

Rockefeller staked his campaign on the one vital issue of Radical Rightism. As early as mid-March, he declared in a press statement in Fresno that Goldwater deserved defeat because the Birch Society was supporting him. Stepping up the velocity of his attack as the primary neared, Rockefeller declared bluntly that Goldwater, if nominated, could not win and that his nomination would be a disaster for the Republican Party. Citing Goldwater's stands on various issues, Rockefeller stressed:

"Certainly this does not add up to responsible Republicanism. Certainly it is not in the mainstream of American thought . . . If the Republican Party follows the road of irresponsibility and extremism, it cannot expect to command the attention, the respect and the support of the American people sufficient to remain a major force in American political life."

Goldwater said relatively little. His campaign aides made no secret of the fact that they were deliberately trying to keep their too talkative candidate under wraps. Press conferences were virtually eliminated; question-and-answer sessions were shunned. Goldwater appeared on television, delivered set and formal speeches, but avoided those encounters with the public that might lead him to pop off and scare the wits out of the voters as he had in New Hampshire. There was just one exception to this tight-lipped, buttoned-up strategy. Goldwater agreed to appear on Howard K. Smith's *Issues and Answers* television program over the ABC network on May 23. Instantly, liberated just this once from his advisers' tight, restraining reins, Goldwater did what came naturally. He shot from the hip.

It all came about without any prodding from Smith, as a free-will offering on Goldwater's part. They were discussing the problems of the war in South Vietnam, and Smith asked casually about the difficulties of interdicting the Communists' jungle supply routes from the North. How could these be cut? Goldwater answered:

"Well, it is not as easy as it sounds, because these are not trails that are out in the open. I have been in these rain forests of Burma and South China. You are perfectly safe wandering through them as far as an enemy hurting you. There have been several suggestions made. I don't think we would use any of them. But defoliation of the forests by low-yield atomic weapons *could well be done*. When you remove the foliage, you remove the cover." (Italics added.)

This atomic defoliation suggestion produced an international uproar. Goldwater partisans like David Lawrence tried to argue that Goldwater had never suggested, never in this world, that atomic bombs actually should be used. He had been merely, in Lawrence's view, discussing something that might conceivably be done. The exact quotes of the television interview convey a much stronger impression than that. Furthermore, this was not the first time that Goldwater's militaristic mind had toyed with the idea of letting go with the atom bomb to settle affairs in South Vietnam. On May 20, 1963, *Newsweek* magazine, commenting on his sometimes "breath-taking simple solutions," quoted him to this effect in discussing South Vietnam: "I'd drop a low-yield atomic bomb on the Chinese supply lines in North Vietnam or maybe shell 'em with the Seventh Fleet." Goldwater's mind, it would seem, had been toying for a long time with the desirability of experimenting with the atomic gadgets in our arsenal; and, with this mental predisposition, his remark to Howard K. Smith just popped out naturally.

Though the dedicated might shout, as they did, that Barry didn't mean it, that Barry had been misquoted again by an inimical press that had distorted his words, the only possible conclusion that a less partisan person can come to is that Goldwater did mean it. And this, indeed, was the way most of the world took it.

The Soviet News Agency, Tass, charged that Goldwater had lacked the courage to say "that the bomb would wipe out everything living from the face of the much-suffering land of South Vietnam. It is to be hoped that sober people would be found in the United States who would bring the crazy Senator to his senses." American reaction was almost as severe. A RAND physicist denounced the idea as "irresponsible." A Nobel Prize nuclear physicist at Berkeley called it "completely ridiculous." The Navy's former chief atomic scientist said: "It reflects ignorance of nuclear weaponry." He pointed out that a 10-kiloton bomb, half the power of the Hiroshima bomb, would blow down 90 percent of the jungle within a range of less than a mile. But the Viet Cong supply routes, he explained, ran for 800 miles through the jungle along the Vietnam frontier. "To clear these hundreds of square miles would require hundreds of bombs," he said. And Dr. George Leppert, noted nuclear scientist at Stanford University, asked: "What about the people? It would be political idiocy to use nuclear weapons for an objective such as the Senator described."

But it was not until later, when Henry Cabot Lodge returned from South Vietnam, that Goldwater was subjected to the crowning ridicule. Lodge in his first press conference pointed out that we were already defoliating trees along the Viet Cong supply routes, but not with atomic bombs—with weed killer.

This lone, but graphic incident of Goldwater hip-shooting, many thought, must certainly turn the tide in the California campaign. But it didn't. One of the reasons that it didn't may be found in the army of zealots, numbering high into the thousands, whom the Birchers enlisted under the Goldwater banner—and in the tactics they used.

Rockefeller subsequently, on Barry Gray's WMCA broadcast of July 5, described in detail the storm-trooper methods of threat and intimidation that were used against his workers in California. He said:

"We had Rockefeller-for-President offices all throughout these counties. They received over 200 bomb threats. Every office got them. The women workers, particularly, would get calls at night—threats, vile language. One of our women delegates almost went to pieces under this kind of pressure. Her car was pushed off the road late at night. These tactics, in my opinion, are very serious as a portent for the future.

"We had a reception given by Leonard Firestone, who was my Southern California chairman. Some of these young Goldwater supporters tried to come in the front door, but were not able to get in because they were carrying these placards and so forth. So they came in the kitchen and up the back way, tore down all our posters. There were about 5,000 people there. They put stuff in the punch—it may have been acid—to spoil it. They went around with their hands and stamping on all the sandwiches.

"Then the leader of this group . . . got in a fight [with a young businessman]. They ended up on the floor. There was a big cigarette ash tray—the kind you see standing in hotels—made of porcelain. That was upset and the businessman was pushed over on it and had to have seven stitches in his arm! . . . This just doesn't seem like America . . . ."

These were the kind of people and these the tactics—

people and tactics that Goldwater was flatly to endorse in his acceptance-speech praise of extremism—that brought him victory in California. Rockefeller came out of the northern counties with a sizable lead, but the Birchite South did him in. Goldwater rolled up a margin of 75,000 votes, defeating Rockefeller by a wafer-thin 1.8 percent of all the votes cast. In the entire 50 states, he had won just one primary—but it was the one he had to have. With California's 86 votes in his pocket, he had un unbreakable grip on the Republican nomination.

CHAPTER XVIII

The Convention

For the eastern Establishment of the Republican Party, there remained only the dying agony. It was an agony that farce was to rob of all dignity.

With defeat in California, Nelson Rockefeller was finished. And he knew it. If Goldwater was to be stopped, someone else would have to stop him.

Desperately, the Eastern Republicans looked around for a champion. There was only one possibility—Governor William Scranton, the personable Governor of Pennsylvania. Scranton, who had little national stature and realized it, had been playing a waiting game, sitting out the battle in a position to pick up the pieces when Rockefeller blocked Goldwater. Rockefeller's failure to throw the block doomed this strategy and left the eastern, more liberal wing of the party with no alternative except to pitch Scranton into the fight.

There was some hope for Scranton. Eisenhower, the hero of Gettysburg, liked him and had encouraged his entry into politics. If Eisenhower could be persuaded to take a definite stand and hold it, his prestige could be a mighty force in halting the Goldwater steamroller. An ideal forum offered. The Governor's Conference was meeting in Cleveland the week following the California primary; if Scranton went there and announced his candidacy with Eisenhower's impressive backing, a counter-boom might well be launched.

For a brief moment, it appeared as if things might work out this way. On Saturday, June 6, the hero of Gettysburg called Scranton to conference, and the Pennsylvania Governor evidently came away feeling that Ike was in his corner. He departed for Cleveland and a Sunday television appearance at which he was scheduled to hurl his bombshell. Before he could do so, he found the bomb fizzling in his hands.

Goldwater's workers had an ace up their sleeves—George

Humphrey, multi-millionaire Ohio steel magnate, Ike's former Secretary of the Treasury, one of the arch-conservative members of the Eisenhower "team" and a man who had always had the ear of the leader. Humphrey was a Goldwater man, and no sooner did it appear that Ike might abandon his characteristic pose of being loftily above all mundane political battles than the telephone wires began to burn and Humphrey got the ear of his former boss. The result was a last-minute call to Scranton in Cleveland. Ike wanted to make it clear, he said, that he did not want to join any last-minute "cabal" to stop Goldwater.

The effect was to stop Scranton in his tracks.

With the Eisenhower power drained from the powerhouse, the Pennsylvania Governor suffered out a miserable, evasive television appearance. The ringing declaration he had come to utter remained hidden and unspoken on a folded piece of paper before him. He mouthed nothings, saying only what all knew—that he was available. The result was a fiasco that turned the Eisenhower halo into mockery (a favorite crack was that Lee did better at Gettysburg) and that left the eastern Republicans with their vaunted stature in tatters.

The on-again, off-again Scranton candidacy soon became definitely on again. Goldwater's announcement that he would vote against the civil rights bill was the deciding factor. Goldwater placed his stand (one indispensable to his candidacy) on the grounds of high principle. He was opposed, he said, to the public accommodations and equal employment sections of the bill. He went further. He feared that these sections "will require for their effective execution the creation of a police state. And so, because I am unalterably opposed to any threats to our system of government and the loss of our God-given liberties, I shall vote 'No' on this bill."

Roy Wilkins, head of the NAACP, subsequently pointed out that Goldwater's stated grounds of opposition and his fear of a "police state" parroted almost word for word the views of Robert Welch as expressed in the Birch Society's *Blue Book* in March. Wilkins, putting the two quotes side by side, asked the NAACP convention in Washington: "Who is following whom?"

Goldwater's declaration against civil rights decided Scranton. On June 12, he went to Baltimore and in a ringing speech before the Maryland State Convention, he declared his candidacy. He had come, he said, to offer his party "a choice" from "the echo of fear, or reaction . . . the echo from the never-never land that puts our nation backward to a lesser place in the world of free men."

Scranton saw the Republican Party—and perhaps the nation—endangered "if we let an exclusion-minded minority dominate our platform and choose our candidates." He was, he said, not ready to have Abraham Lincoln read out of the Republican Party.

It was a good speech, but words were pitiful and ineffectual weapons with which to counter the power of brute power. And brute power was what Goldwater wielded at San Francisco.

The platform committee, the entire machinery of the convention was in his hands and the hands of his fanatical followers. In the East, as the Republicans assembled in San Francisco in that second week of July, 1964, there were still the incorrigible optimists; there were still those that thought "something would happen" simply because they thought it had to. One heard repeated, time and again: "Remember what happened to Taft in 1952." Taft, too, had gone into the convention with more than enough delegates to ensure the nomination, only to see them melt away under eastern pressure and join the Eisenhower battalions. But 1964 was not 1952; and what such optimistic speculations failed to take into account was that there were new forces at work and that they were about to seize control of the Republican Party.

In 1952, Thomas E. Dewey and his Eastern architects of the Eisenhower crusade had been able to wield the club of enormous economic power over all but the most committed Taft delegates. They had been able to marshal behind them the enormous power of the Chase Manhattan Bank, the Rockefellers and their far-flung interests, U.S. Steel, Ford Motors and other mighty and moderate industrialists. Telephone calls could be made threatening to cut off deposits or institute other economic reprisals if Taft delegates did not switch to Eisenhower. This was brutal pressure, the exercise of the raw power that lurks behind the veneer of platform politics—and it worked. But it could work no longer.

Goldwater had eastern money, but he did not depend on it. He represented a new force—the suddenly burgeoning and supremely powerful economic dynasties of the South, the Southwest and the West. This was wildcat oil money, fantastic millions piled up with the aid of the 27½ percent depletion allowance that had created a specially favored class of citizens. This was space age and warfare state money

—the profits amassed from the five space centers that sprawl in a "missile crescent" across the South and Southwest and boast annual budgets of $3.5 billion; the enormous profits derived from the $6 billion a year in military procurement contracts that pour into the state of California. This was the kind of money that had financed Joe McCarthy, that had seen in Barry Goldwater a personable and charming and more powerful McCarthy. It was money that belonged to the white Protestant country-club set, western-oriented, not knowing and little caring about the problems of the eastern urban centers, the plight of immigrants and minority groups, the struggle of the Negro for equality. Its bias was shown—and it could hardly have been by accident—in the composition of the huge Goldwater bloc of delegates and alternates from California; there wasn't a Negro or a Jew among them.

This was new power, the emergence of a new force on the political scene, and it was a power so domineering it could well swing the entire nation by the tail. The very identity of the money men who raised an estimated $3.5 million for Goldwater's primary effort—a figure exceeding the $3 million goal envisioned in the first meeting in Chicago in 1962— showed how the power was concentrated. A few were from the East, but the real muscle was supplied by the Western reaches of the country. Daniel C. Gainey, owner of Josten's Inc., a multi-million-dollar Minnesota printing, engraving and bookbinding business, headed the Goldwater fund drive. Three of the eleven men on the finance committee were oilmen. The "finance committee locator list" included such names as these: Richard Kleberg, of the enormous King Ranch in Texas; Robert Carter, of Continental Airlines; Charles Barr, the Standard Oil of Indiana representative at Chicago in 1962; Joseph Pew, of the Sun Oil interests; Charlton Lyons, the oil man who ran for Governor of Louisiana; J. Symington Fife and G. R. Herberge, retailers who operate a large chain of stores in the Upper Midwest. This was the team, these the kind of men who raised $1.5 million in California alone for Goldwater's campaign there; and when, in the closing days, more heavy cash was needed for a saturation TV blitz, Goldwater's aides took to the telephones and in two days obtained from out-of-state backers another $200,000. What such a feat says is that the Eastern financial powers, the "King Makers" of the past, had been out-performed in their own special bailiwick—the realm of hard cash. They had lost their handle on the deliberations of the party; they could no longer exert decisive leverage.

As Walter Lippmann had written so perceptively six months earlier, what Goldwater really represented was not conservatism, but the hard rightism of "the newly rich on the make."

The extremes to which these new forces were prepared to go was demonstrated time and again at San Francisco. And this despite the fact that the delegates and the galleries were on their good behavior because all the battles that mattered had been fought and won before the convention even convened. There was no need for storm-trooper tactics, but still the unmistakable impression was conveyed that Goldwater fanatics could play very rough indeed.

When one Negro delegate refused to join a Goldwater demonstration, he suddenly discovered, as the paraders passed a second time, that his jacket had been set on fire. When James Brophy and family bolted the Georgia delegation for Scranton, they were greeted with snarls: "You're nigger lovers—Communists." One Southern Goldwater delegate (who later denied he had said it) was quoted as declaring: "Lee Oswald should have got the Congressional Medal of Honor." Another Goldwater delegate told Stewart Alsop: "If Scranton gets it, there'll be blood three feet deep on the Cow Palace floor, and the nomination won't be worth the powder to blow it to hell." Hard-featured private eyes guarded Goldwater's suite and were even stationed on the fire escape. When Mary Scranton tried to descend the fire escape to her husband's offices below Goldwater's, they turned her back. Later, after the Goldwater nomination, when she left the Cow Palace and went down a ramp to join her husband in a waiting trailer, the ramp suddenly burst into flames behind her—and police said they suspected arson. About it all, as Drew Pearson reported, was "the smell of fascism," and Governor Brown was later to declare that Goldwater's acceptance speech, with its plain endorsement of extremism, had about it "the stench of fascism."

Even in the more deliberative deeds on the convention floor, the storm-trooper mentality showed. Former President Eisenhower, having flipped and flopped back and forth, managing always by some new ineptitude to cut the ground out from under the Scranton forces he was supposed secretly to favor, made one of the more sober and high-level speeches of the convention. But in the course of it, stung by criticisms of his vacillation, he took occasion to denounce partisan columnists and television commentators who thought they knew everything. Instantly—and to his somewhat obvious surprise—the hall erupted in thunderous applause. A cardinal faith of Goldwaterism is that its hero always looks so bad in the press because the press twists and distorts what he says. And so, when Eisenhower touched this sensitive chord, the convention broke out in wild applause, and many of the Goldwater cohorts stood and jeered and shook their fists at newspaper and television reporters. Hitler's fanatics burned books lest the truth might prevail, and one got the indelible impression that some of Goldwater's would like to lynch newsmen.

Then there was the night that Nelson Rockefeller, closing out a consistently courageous performance, led the fight to get the Goldwater-dictated platform altered to include a specific condemnation of such extremist groups as the Communist Party, the Ku Klux Klan and the Birchers. The Goldwater management of the convention deliberately stalled by reading every word of the windy party platform, eating up time so that most of the television viewers back East would have gone to bed before Rockefeller was permitted in range of the cameras. The New York governor had been allotted just five minutes to make his point, and he had hardly started to speak, denouncing extremism in any form, when he was interrupted by a storm of boos and organized shouting from the floor. "We want Barry! We want Barry!" a well-drilled claque kept shouting in unison. Rockefeller stood there, facing them down, his broad face creased in a taunting grin, just as if he were saying to the "kooks"—"Go ahead, you're proving my point for me." Chairman Thruston Morton rapped for order, and Rockefeller jabbed at him, too. "Go ahead and control these people," he told Morton. "That's your job." Still the "kooks" would not be quiet, would not let Rockefeller be heard if they could help it. He was interrupted some twenty times, was told his time was up. He refused to leave the podium. "I haven't finished my speech," he said. "It's not my fault if you can't control these people." And finish he did, his point well made with the help of his unruly audience.

The Goldwater steamroller rolled ruthlessly over every liberal objection to its platform. In addition to the condemnation of extremism, the liberals wanted to insert a declaration that would give more than palest lip service to civil rights, and they wanted to write into the platform a specific provision that control of nuclear weapons must at all times be retained in the civilian hands of the President of the United States. These proposals were all buried under an avalanche of Goldwater votes, and it became clear that Goldwater had such an iron grip on this convention that nothing could shake it. Not even another graphic example of Goldwater hip-shooting.

On June 30 Goldwater had given a long interview to a reporter from the German magazine *Der Spiegel*, and *Der Spiegel* hit the stands just as the Republicans were hitting San Francisco. The timing gave special emphasis to some especially revealing Goldwater quotes—quotes that exposed again the rigidly militaristic bent of his mind.

Goldwater's *Der Spiegel* performance must be assessed against the background of his previous pronouncements. Time and again, he had decried civilian control of the military, a cardinal principle of the American system from the time of the founding fathers. He had shouted that he feared the civilians more than the military because they were taking over; he had attacked McNamara's civilian control of the Defense Department in such intemperate terms that Detroit industrialists had thought him "whey." Now, in his interview with *Der Spiegel*, he commented that Germany would have won both World Wars I and II if the military had been allowed to run things, if the civilians hadn't interfered. Goldwater indicated to *Der Spiegel* that he, as President, would make no such mistakes. He said:

"I would make it abundantly clear . . . that we aren't going to pull out of Southeast Asia. But that we are going to win in fact.

"Now the next decision becomes based on military decisions. I don't think that's up to a Presidential candidate or even a President. I would turn to my Joint Chiefs of Staff and say, 'Fellows, we made the decision to win, now it's your problem.'"

Clearly, the President would become little more than a figurehead, a yes-man for the military; if the Joint Chiefs wanted to press the atomic button, they could.

Equally disturbing to at least some sections of the American public and to many of our allies abroad was another passage revelatory of Goldwater's fanatical belief we are engaged in a holy war against communism. A mind nurtured by Robert Welch and Fred Schwarz and Billy James Hargis seemed incapable of understanding that the world has always been a complex of different and frequently inimical ideologies, that no one faith or system has ever been able to dominate all. To Goldwater, quite obviously, the holy wars of the Middle Ages, which settled nothing, must be repeated in the nuclear age when they would settle everything. This was the passage:

"This struggle today is a struggle between Godless people

and the people of God, and if you want to put it in its basic form, it's between slavery and freedom. It's now world-wide. I claim that we cannot live with these two philosophies in the world forever. Sometime there'll be only one. We're not fighting the Russian people, we're not fighting the Red Chinese people. Our conflict is a conflict between governments and government philosophies."

Goldwater's holy war-military fixations led him almost inevitably to envision a foreign policy that would be a risky exercise in brinkmanship. He told *Der Spiegel*:

"Any foreign policy that this country adopts should not be afraid of war. This is brinkmanship . . . ."

Hopping on these pronouncements, Governor Scranton called a press conference in which he said, quite justifiably: "The reckless comments of the Senator from Arizona in the area of war and peace have now become a matter of grave national concern."

Perhaps. But obviously they were not a matter of great concern to already roped and tied Goldwater delegates in San Francisco. Nothing could sway them or cause them for a moment to doubt. Amid the usual convention hoopla, the nominating speeches were duly made, and on July 15, on the first ballot, Goldwater buried Scranton by a vote of 883 to 214. Scranton then took the platform and urged that the verdict be made unanimous. The following night, in routine fashion, the convention underwrote Goldwater's choice for his running mate—Rep. William E. Miller, a hard conservative from upstate New York—and the stage was set for Goldwater's acceptance speech.

He entered the hall to a storm of applause and the strains of "The Battle Hymn of the Republic," a refrain that, perhaps only co-incidentally, is the favorite marching song of the Birchers. In this atmosphere of evangelistic Americanism, Goldwater gave a speech full of rousing generalities, barren of any suggestion of specifics.

Communism, he proclaimed, must be made to "give way to the forces of freedom"—but he did not say, if communism is so stupid as to object, how this might be accomplished.

He saw possible "tyranny" in "the failure of public officials to keep the streets safe from bullies and marauders," an oblique reference to Negro demonstrators and rioters—but he did not indicate what he, as an ardent advocate of states' rights and a man who shuddered at the first whiff of a police state, could possibly do to correct a situation wholly within the police domain of the localities and the states.

He envisioned a utopian world in which "this Atlantic civilization" would galvanize and guide the emergent nations; in which "the whole world of Europe" would be "reunified and free"—but he did not indicate, of course, how all of this might be accomplished.

It was a speech that stirred the faithful to mild outbursts of applause, but one that did not really send them until the final passages, in which Goldwater virtually read out of the party any who did not want to go his way. He said:

"Anyone who joins us in all sincerity we welcome. Those, those who do not care for our cause, we don't expect to enter our ranks in any case. And let our Republicanism so focused and so dedicated not be made fuzzy and futile by unthinking and stupid labels.

"I would remind you that extremism in defense of liberty is no vice!

"And let me remind you also that moderation in the pursuit of justice is no virtue!"

Those two lines, heavily underlined in his script by Goldwater himself (he had confided to aides that he really admired them), sparked the tinder in the Cow Palace, and touched off a true blaze of applause.

The statement and the reaction serve as the best possible epitaph to the Republican National Convention of 1964.

CHAPTER XIX

The Candidate and the Campaign

The Goldwater campaign of 1964 almost certainly will pivot about three main features—the personality of its leader, the fanaticism of his Radical Right followers from whom by exercise of personality he will try to set himself apart, and the white backlash whose ultimate influence, at this writing, no man can estimate.

Of these three elements, the Goldwater personality, with its schizophrenic split between mannerism and mind, will be used like gold in the bank by his brain trust. The manner of the man—the handsome appearance, the engaging smile, the charming and seemingly modest self-deprecation of his own talents and ambitions—makes him a natural television star; and his aides, in the planning immediately after the convention, made no secret of the fact that heavy television exposure, a feature of every Goldwater campaign, would be relied upon to project their candidate to the people in his most likeable guise.

The split-personality aspect of Goldwater becomes, therefore, central to the campaign, and it is important to understand it. Stewart Alsop of *The Saturday Evening Post* put it this way:

"Goldwater does not look or act like the leader of a revolt, and this may be the secret of the Goldwater phenomenon. He is a rather diffident man, visibly distressed by the fake-genial hurly-burly of campaign, and his humor is as self-deprecating as Adlai Stevenson's. . . . Even when he 'shoots from the hip' —when he remarks, for example, that the 'jackassian' decisions of the Supreme Court are 'not necessarily the law of the land,' or that in Vietnam 'defoliation of the forests by low-yield atomic weapons could well be done'—his tone is one of sweet reason, as though any reasonable man could be expected to adhere to such sensible views. The sweet reason of his manner may explain in part why all the disparate forces of the extreme right, from racists to Birchites, have coalesced around Goldwater, like bees swarming around a queen. If Goldwater sounded like a demagogue, he would be a mere fringe politician. But because the whole style of the man belies extremism, he has proved to be an ideal leader of extremists."

The problem of the Goldwater campaign is going to be one of projecting *charisma* at the expense of thought—of making lovable and reasonable-seeming Barry appeal to Everyman without scaring the pants off Everyman by giving him too close a glimpse of what lovable and reasonable-seeming Barry actually stands for. Yet such glimpses are essential if the American voter is to make a sensible choice between reason and unreason.

The qualities of mind that contrast so sharply with the smooth veneer of manner and appearance show perhaps more vividly in trivial incidents than even in his major hip-shooting performances. These incidents, spontaneous and unstudied, keep niggling at the mind of one who has tried to study Goldwater.

Take his military fixation. Calm, reasonable-seeming on television, Goldwater can be a trigger-happy terror with a gun in his hands. During the war, when he first flew in a gunnery exercise at the Gila Bend Range near Phoenix, he aimed his plane, armed with a 20-caliber cannon, straight at the target, dove low, and pressed the trigger so hard and continuously that the magazine was exhausted in one furious burst of flame. The target was literally blown to bits, and the gun barrel became so overheated it almost melted and had to be replaced. Couple this with Jack Bell's discovery that "Goldwater reads and re-reads Karl von Clausewitz' *On War*, with its exposition of total destruction of the enemy by any available means"; think of both these things in a frame of reference that includes all of Goldwater's militant pronouncements about brinkmanship and defoliating the Vietnam forests and causing "a little shooting" war in Cuba—and one can hardly feel comfortable at the thought that here is the man to whom Americans might entrust the decision of peace or war and the custody of nuclear bombs.

Most Americans in this jittery age when nuclear holocaust hovers around the corner, waiting for the spark of some ill-considered or impulsive action, will probably be seeking in November a President who conveys strength without hysteria. They will be seeking for those tell-tale signs of calmness and common sense and sound judgment—that indefinable "balance" which, in this day and age, is so vital in a leader. To many, the Goldwater who appears on television may seem like such a man. His surface manner, as Stewart Alsop noted, conveys well this sense of calm reasonableness. But, again, tell-tale incidents stick in the mind, little things that seem to say this is a much harder and more arrogant and more temperamental man than appears on the surface.

Take the night of May 1, 1964 in Atlanta, Georgia. Goldwater flew in to be greeted by a wildly cheering crowd of the faithful. Apparently, he hadn't expected such a reception; he was tired and out of sorts. He pushed his way brusquely through the crowd, refusing to speak to them. When a little girl tried to put a big white hat on his head, he pushed it back and said: "I don't want that." He arrived at last at his car, turned and paused as if to speak; and Don Baird, of Station WSB, shoved a microphone up close. Goldwater slapped it away and snapped: "Get that damned thing out of here." He added: "I don't like people pointing microphones in my face." Then he said to the crowd that he hadn't expected such a reception; he was sorry to disappoint them— and he got in his car and left. It was, perhaps, a trivial incident, but one that seemed to hint at quite a different man than the Barry Goldwater you are likely to see on television.

More serious and even more revealing was the teapot-tempest that erupted in September, 1962, when a student at the University of Colorado wrote for a student publication a long, rambling and injudicious attack on Goldwater. The victim of youthful enthusiasm and bad judgment, the student called Goldwater "a mountebank" and "no better than a common criminal." Officials at the university were horrified and acted immediately. Quigg Newton, the university president, ordered an investigation. The editor who had let the unwarranted and libelous phrases get into print was removed; the student-author was threatened with expulsion; and Newton telegraphed Goldwater a profound apology. This, it seemed should have ended the matter, but it didn't. Goldwater saw, not a youthful indiscretion but some dark conspiracy, and fired back in a telegram to Newton:

"I have spoken with groups of some 250 colleges and schools in this country, and this is the only one where the Socialists, or whatever you care to call them, seem to have the ability to do what they want without censure. I must because of this, then, come to the conclusion that you either do not know what is going on in the university or you don't care, and in charity, I will presume the former. To put it briefly, I doubt that you have the interest or the concern to be in the position you hold."

Such an attack on a university president over such a trifling incident seems hardly worthy of a U. S. Senator—and especially one aspiring to the Presidency. As the Kentucky *Journal* commented, "a case of juvenile bad manners has given Senator Goldwater a case of rather ugly adult bad temper." And the Arizona *Journal* added: "An obscure student went too far. We all learn something then. But an important man in Washington went too far, also. And we learn something from that, too."

We learn enough to wonder whether such a man could keep calm and cool if, as President, he should be entrusted with the awesome responsibilities of the nuclear age.

Frightening as are some of these qualities of Goldwater, those of his fanatical followers are more alarming still. We have used for years a deceptive term. We have called such extremists "the lunatic fringe," a description that implies they are lesser rabble who don't amount to much. In today's America, unfortunately, this is a decidedly false perspective. The "kooks" are not just the young, the illiterate and "the little old women in tennis shoes"; they include a heavy swatch of millionaires and highly placed Respectables.

Shortly after the Goldwater nomination, a businessman returned from a trip to Southern California. He regarded himself as a strong conservative, but he came back shocked and stunned by the ultra-conservative frenzy he had witnessed. He had had a conference with a powerful businessman, the kingpin of an important firm; and he had found that, before he could even begin to talk business, he had to listen to a half-hour's oration on the virtues of Goldwater:

"He talked as if this was the Second Coming. He made no bones about it that if we didn't act—and act now—the hammer-and-sickle might be flying over the White House next week. He was clear about what they were going to do; they were going to save the nation; they were going to clean this up—and you better not get in their way because they were going to roll right over you if you did. I just stood there and listened and didn't say a word. There wasn't any use. You couldn't talk to him.

"He had this all wrapped up in the folds of the flag. And what are you going to do? Go out and fight the flag?"

Goldwater, who has restored his consistency on one score by withdrawing from the Senatorial race in Arizona and concentrating on the Presidential campaign, is certainly going to wave that flag.

In July, 1964, the *Liberty Letter*, mailed from 300 Independence Avenue S.E., Washington, D.C., carried this headline: SECRET LBJ TREATY DANGEROUS RED PLOT. The newsletter told its readers that "the latest Johnson dealings with the Reds has produced a Consular Treaty" which the tainted Democratic administration would try to sneak through the Senate. The *Liberty Letter* contained phrases like "Johnson and his friends at the State Department CANNOT establish this espionage network for the Soviet Union" without the approval of the Senate which "must become the battlefield again where patriots can resist." This drivel was being sent out by Goldwater backers in envelopes decorated with Barry Goldwater trading stamps.

Such propaganda makes it clear that the campaign of 1964 almost certainly will be pitched at two levels, just as Barry Goldwater himself is a two-level man. Goldwater will take the high ground, unless he escapes from his palace guard and begins hip-shooting again. The dedicated fanatics who represent his hard-core political strength will try by every devious tactic known to man to impugn the loyalty of every Democrat and to bring into the corral all the white back-lashers, all the bigots. It will be a campaign worthy on both levels of the Phoenix Country Club McCarthy.

Other Black Cat Books

TRAIN TO PAKISTAN. A novel by Kushwant Singh   BA-1 50¢
The passionate love story of a Sikh boy and Muslim girl, set in turbulent India. "A brew of brimstone, blood and nitric acid served piping hot."—*American Scholar*

CAIN'S BOOK. A novel by Alexander Trocchi   BA-2 50¢
"The genuine article on a dope addict's life," wrote the *N. Y. Herald Tribune.* "Just slightly less graphic than Henry Miller," added the *Library Journal.* A candid, ruthlessly honest portrayal of the tortured half-world of drugs and addicts.

JAZZ: ITS EVOLUTION AND ESSENCE by André Hodeir BB-3 60¢
Undoubtedly the best and most perceptive book on jazz ever written. "The most penetrating book of its kind."—*New Yorker*

THE FOLKLORE OF SEX by Albert Ellis   BC-4 75¢
An irreverent, revealing dissection of American sexual habits, including extramarital relations, petting, preversions, etc. "Ranks among the important contributions to life and love in the U.S.A."—*American Journal of Psychotherapy*

ON LOVE AND SEXUALITY by Dr. Edrita Fried   BC-5 75¢
A modern, frank approach to sexual apathy, frigidity, boredom, homosexuality, clinging, masturbation, promiscuity, and other problems of self-adjustment.

MUST YOU CONFORM? by Robert Lindner   BB-6 60¢
A challenge to America, and to the demon of conformity, by the brilliant psychoanalyst Robert Lindner, author of *The Fifty-Minute Hour* and *Rebel Without a Cause.*

DRUGS AND THE MIND by Robert S. de Ropp   BC-7 75¢
Whether you smoke, drink, take tranquilizers or have ever been tempted by any of the pills or drugs offered as a short cut to happiness, this book will delight and fascinate you.

RED STAR OVER CHINA by Edgar Snow   RD-8 95¢
The classic, first-hand account of the early years of Chinese Communism, describing the rulers of present-day China, how they took over, etc. Indispensable for an understanding of China today.

LADY CHATTERLEY'S LOVER. A novel by D. H. Lawrence BA-9 50¢
Available to American readers after 31 years of suppression. "Ulysses apart, this is the most notorious novel of the 20th Century, prosecuted from Poland to Japan. . . ."—*New Republic*

TROPIC OF CANCER. A novel by Henry Miller BD-10 95¢

The complete, unexpurgated Grove Press edition. "For me *Tropic of Cancer* stands beside Moby Dick. . . . American literature today begins and ends with the meaning of what Miller has done."—Lawrence Durrell

MAN AGAINST AGING by Robert S. de Ropp BC-11 75¢

The fascinating story of man's efforts to understand aging and to prolong life and vitality, complete with the most recent scientific information, brilliantly written in clear, non-technical style.

ALCOHOL by Berton Roueché BA-12 50¢

A famed medical reporter presents the whole history of fermented and distilled beverages. "A 100-proof volume filled with fact and lore. . . . You will enjoy reading it, with or without a drink."—*Los Angeles Times*

MASOCHISM IN SEX AND SOCIETY by Theodor Reik BD-13 95¢

The most frequent and significant of all perversions—man as a pain-seeking animal—is discussed in this extremely readable and enlightening book. "Reik is undoubtedly the best living writer about psychoanalysis. . . ."—*N. Y. Times Book Review*

UNDERSTANDING YOUR CHILD by Dr. Edith Buxbaum BA-14 50¢

For all parents: an indispensable guidebook in the elements of child psychology. "The book is simply written and yet no compromise is made on the solidity of scientific observation. It can be put in the hands of mothers at all levels of educational and sociological background."—*Parents' Magazine*

ANTI-SEMITE AND JEW by Jean-Paul Sartre BA-15 50¢

The French philosopher's perceptive, scathing portrait of prejudice demonstrates that bigotry is a manifestation of the mediocre mind. "One of the most brilliant psychological analyses of the . . . fanatic anti-Semite which has ever been published."—*Sidney Hook*

THE MIND OF THE MURDERER by Dr. M. Guttmacher BB-16 60¢

Drawn from three decades of courtroom experience, this is a comprehensive description of the genus "murderer." "Capsule stories of murder in the raw that pale much comparable fiction."—*The Saturday Review*

THE HOLY BARBARIANS by Lawrence Lipton BC-17 75¢

Sympathetic and intimate account of the "Beats," delving into the midnight world of sex, drugs, and jazz to extract the meaning of their revolt. The complete story of the generation of hip, cool, and frantic new Bohemians who are turning the American scale of values inside out.

CUBA: Tragedy in Our Hemisphere
                    by Maurice Zeitlin and Robert Scheer BD-55 95¢
A completely new, documented factual appraisal of the history
of Cuba since the revolution that overthrew Batista, and of
America's relations with the new government. It answers the
question everyone is asking: Why has the U.S. come to the
brink of thermonuclear war over Cuba?

FREEDOM RIDE by James Peck   BA-56 50¢
This is a personal report of the rides that made history, showing American idealism at its best and American brutality at
its worst. The detailed coverage of trips to the South reveals the
unflinching courage displayed by Freedom Riders in meeting
violence with non-violence. The foreword is by James Baldwin,
and the introduction by Lillian Smith.

SUMMER STORM by Juan Garcia Hortelano   BC-57 75¢
Winner of the $10,000 International Formentor Prize, this
novel is an extraordinary story of life in a sex-obsessed, guilt-
ridden summer colony for Spain's idle rich, where the mystery
of a dead girl's body explodes the complacency. "A first rate
tale of semi-decadent society."—*New York Herald Tribune*

THE NEW LIFE:
      A Day on a Collective Farm by Fyodor Abramov BA-58 50¢
"A startling indictment of the apathy, discontent and frustrat-
ing failure of collective farm life . . ."—*Time*. This novel is
"one of the most striking and revealing documents to appear
in Russia since the death of Stalin."—David Floyd, *The
Listener*

TROPIC OF CAPRICORN by Henry Miller   BD-59 95¢
The complete and unexpurgated Grove Press edition of the
companion volume to *Tropic of Cancer* has been acclaimed by
critics. The novel takes the reader through Miller's young days
in New York. "Incomparably the finest comic fantasy by any
writer now among the living."—*Newsweek*